HARMONY

Translated from the French
Original title: **L'HARMONIE**

Omraam Mikhaël Aïvanhov

HARMONY

3rd edition

Complete Works – Volume 6 AN

PROSVETA

© Copyright Prosveta S.A. 2001. All rights reserved for all countries. No part of this publication may be reproduced, translated, adapted, stored in a retrieval system or transmitted, whether privately or otherwise, in any form or by any means, electronic, mechanical, photocopying, audio-visual or otherwise, without the prior permission of author and publishers (Law of March 1957 revised).

Prosveta S.A – B.P.12 – 83601 Fréjus CEDEX (France)
ISBN 2-85566-811-5
1st edition: ISBN 2-85566-097-1
original edition: ISBN 2-85566-406-3

Readers will better understand certain aspects of the lectures published in the present volume if they bear in mind that Master Omraam Mikhaël Aïvanhov's teaching was exclusively oral and that the editors have made every effort to respect the flavour and style of each lecture.

The Master's teaching is more than a body of doctrines; it is an organic whole, and his way of presenting it was to approach it from countless different points of view. By treating certain aspects in many different contexts he constantly reveals a new dimension of the whole, and at the same time throws new light on the individual aspects and their vital links with each other.

Omraam Mikhaël Aïvanhov

TABLE OF CONTENTS

I	Harmony	11
II	Medical Science Must be Based on Initiatic Science	39
III	The Future of Medicine	67
IV	A Disciple Must Develop His Spiritual Senses	79
V	What Can We Learn From a House?	103
VI	How Thought is Materialized on the Physical Plane	125
VII	Meditation	147
VIII	The Human Intellect and Cosmic Intelligence	165
IX	The Solar Plexus and the Brain	189
X	The Hara Centre	209
XI	The Initiatic Heart	237
XII	The Aura	253

Chapter One

HARMONY

I

A few moments ago, as I was eating some almonds, I thought what a good idea it would be to plant a whole orchard of almond trees here, at the Bonfin[1]. In the first place, the soil is ideal because almond trees can grow in arid ground; they don't need much water but, more importantly, almonds are very rich in nutrients. They even contain certain elements that combat cancer. For this reason it would be good to be able to eat at least three a day. Some of you might object that you would be tired of them within a week: but you can always grind them up and add a spoonful or two to your salads or your soup, then you would not get sick of them.

So we must plant some almond trees; and then, every year, when the brothers and sisters leave the Bonfin, they can take home bags and bags of almonds to nibble when they are back in their own little corner! We have several acres of land available.

---

[1] 'The Bonfin' is the name of a property near Fréjus on the French Riviera. The members of the Universal White Brotherhood gather here in their hundreds every summer, to study the Teaching of the Universal White Brotherhood, dispensed in the daily lectures of the Master Omraam Mikhaël Aïvanhov, and to put it into practice in all their activities as they work, pray, sing and eat together.

Of course, it has not been cleared yet, but that can soon be done, and if some of the brothers were willing to plant some almond trees they would find it very pleasant, very poetic work.

We have not been very lucky with our almonds this year: the frost killed most of them. Only the trees in my own garden were not damaged by frost, but even they did not produce much. And that is a pity: the biggest almonds I have ever seen grow in my garden, but they were not very plentiful this year. It was the same thing for the olives. Well, there are years like that. It is something that occurs in every area; in fact it occurs for every person, too: the years of plenty alternate with years of famine, the seven fat cows alternate with the seven lean and hungry cows!

While I am on the subject of almonds, let me begin by speaking of something that I have often noticed: a lot of people buy almonds (and walnuts, hazel-nuts and peanuts, too, for that matter) that have already been shelled. Of course, it is much more convenient: they are lighter and easier to deal with, but I don't recommend it at all. You never know how long they have been shelled and they have certainly lost all their etheric particles and, consequently, all vitality, as well as most of their flavour and all nutritional value. It is as though you were eating dead bodies. For certain fruits and vegetables the situation is different: whole rice, for instance, or wheat or beans retain their flavour and nutritional qualities because they have an inner skin. But it is better not to buy your nuts already shelled.

Let me add that you should not eat fruit or vegetables that were picked a long time before, either; they, too, have wilted and are already dead. You pay less for them, that is true, but, in fact, they cost more because you get no life from them. And it is life that counts, life that is more important than anything else. If you have life you have all the rest, too, for part of that life becomes intelligence, another part becomes love, another part activity, will, energy and so on. Whereas when life diminishes you gradually lose all your powers and faculties. People would get along a lot better if only they acquired the habit of counting more on life and less on externals.

And now, why do almonds help to counteract cancer? Because the elements they contain are arranged in perfect harmony, and this harmony prevents cancer – which is the result of anarchy and disorder – from invading the body. The more the spirit of anarchy prevails in the world, therefore, the more this disease will spread. Medical science does not know this, nor does it know that every disease results from a weakness or vice within man himself. It is human beings, themselves, who create diseases. When there is too much nervous tension, one kind of illness appears; excessive sensuality produces another kind of illness; when disharmony increases, yet another kind of illness appears. Every illness is the result of a specific type of disorder, and cancer is the result of anarchy. To guard against cancer, therefore, we have to work at harmony, think about harmony every day, ensure that we are in harmony with the whole of mankind, the whole universe. Of course, I know that no one is capable of living perpetually in a state of perfect harmony, but you can always be conscious and vigilant, so that, if you find that you have slipped back into disharmony, you can get a grip on yourself and reverse the situation again. You must never allow yourself to harbour a climate of disharmony for long, for it spreads into all your cells, cuts off all communication, all currents, all circulation, until your organism can no longer resist the disorder.

Nowadays, this is exactly what is happening: the spirit of anarchy is deliberately cultivated and nurtured all over the world. It is almost as though there were schools in which people learned how to disrupt society by inciting others to anger and a spirit of revolt. The forces of darkness are at work, it is they that are responsible for this diabolical work. Some countries, instead of propagating the viruses of disease – because they would be condemned by others for waging biological warfare – have chosen to propagate the virus of discontent and revolt. And the result is cancer! All anarchists and rebels against society are unwitting carriers of the disease. The Initiatic orders, on the other hand, which work for the reign of peace, harmony and brotherhood so that all men may come to understand, love and be united with their fellows, are propagating germs that eradicate the germs of cancer. If these Initiatic centres did not exist, the whole of humanity would suffer from cancer. I know that very few people will accept this notion. They will say, 'What on earth is he talking about? There is no connection between anarchy and cancer. No biologist thinks so, anyway!' Well, let them rely on the opinion of biologists, if they like! I am only telling you the truth: cancer is the result of the anarchy which is so widespread in the world today. This is why, every day from morning to night, we must work for harmony.

Although I have accepted to talk to you about harmony, I realize that it is going to be very difficult for you to understand me. Not intellectually, of course, but in depth, with your whole being. Human beings are not interested in harmony: everything in their lives contributes to involving them in occupations and activities that are far removed from harmony. Very far, in particular, from harmony as the Initiates conceive of it! But still... try to listen attentively to what I am saying.

Every good thing is contained in harmony: health, strength, fulfilment, happiness, light, inspiration and all the rest. Harmony is poetry, music, painting, sculpture, dance. The whole universe, all perfections, all qualities and all virtues, is included in this one thing: harmony. Those who sow disorder, therefore, will inevitably be destroyed and obliterated one day, because they are working with negative, hostile, destructive forces. Once and for all, you must make up your minds to learn the laws of Nature, but you must also learn how man is constructed and what his relations must be with those laws.

If you are interested in your own happiness and fulfilment you must think about harmony; work to bring yourself into harmony with the whole universe. If you persevere at this, the day will come when you will feel that your whole being, from the tips of your toes to the top of your head, is in communion and vibrating in unison with Cosmic Life. When this moment comes – not before – you will understand what life, creation and love are; before that, it is not possible to understand. Intellectually, outwardly, you may imagine that you have understood, but no: genuine understanding cannot be gained through the activity of a few brain cells. It is the whole being, the whole body that must understand: even your feet, your arms, your stomach and liver... True understanding involves every cell of your body. Understanding is a sensation: you feel something and then you know it, you understand it because you have tasted it.

No amount of intellectual understanding can compare to the understanding of sensation. When you experience love, hatred, anger or sorrow, you know what it is. If you say that you know what love is, without ever having been in love, you are lying! But if you have truly experienced love, then you know what it is. You may be unable to explain or express it, but you know it: that is true knowledge. Knowledge is to vibrate in unison with all that exists. When your whole body vibrates in unison with a truth, a sensation or an object, you know that truth, sensation or object. This is why the essential preoccupation of a disciple must be to attune himself to the heavenly hierarchies so as to vibrate in unison with them. If he works for this harmony night and day, he will, one day, experience sensations beautiful and precious beyond words.

I have often thought of giving you a whole series of lectures about nothing but this one word, 'harmony'; about all that it stands for in every area. Compared to the vast numbers of those who work for destruction and create mountains of difficulties and darkness, there is no more than a handful of human beings in the world who understand that we must unite and work in harmony in order to counter the ills that threaten humanity: war, poverty and disease. This tiny minority is not mighty enough to combat the bad influence of the majority. I have always said that numbers are extremely important: the numbers of those who are good, pure, enlightened and capable of taking part in the formation of a universal brotherhood whose decisions would have some weight in world affairs. Instead of understanding and uniting in this work of transformation, instead of collaborating in this tremendous work, most human beings choose to be individualistic and remain isolated, separate. They work only for their own interests.

For example, if the brothers who come and plant the almond trees we were talking about earlier, worked for some kind of reward or because they wanted to be thanked and admired, they would not be disinterested. True spiritualists[2] work for a divine idea and it is this idea that is their reward, for it is directly linked to Heaven; it is a world in itself. They work for an idea and that idea assumes the responsibility for giving them joy, enthusiasm and hope in return. If you do not work for a divine idea, even if you get a very good salary, you will not receive joy or happiness, because you will not have this link with Heaven. But if you work for a divine idea, even if no one ever says thank you or acknowledges what you do, you will always feel fulfilled. This is something you must understand. Plant a divine idea in your head, work for a divine idea, and you will see what that idea can do for you: it will improve your whole existence, it will even prolong your life.

Personally, that is what I do: I work for an idea. If I am different from most people, it is not that I am more intelligent, richer or more knowledgeable. No, there are a great many who are far more gifted in these areas; it is simply that I work for an idea. But how difficult it is to get people to understand the power and efficacy of an idea, to understand that it is alive, that it is active! And yet, believe me, nothing is more potent or more

---

[2] The word 'spiritualist', in the language of Omraam Mikhaël Aïvanhov, simply means one who looks at things from a spiritual point of view, whose philosophy of life is based on belief in a spiritual reality.

stimulating than a divine idea! I am speaking from experience. In fact, everything I tell you is drawn from my own experience.

A great many people who come to the Brotherhood are very diligent and ardent as long as they think that there is some knowledge to be gleaned from my talks or they have a hope of getting to know some pretty girls. But once they have got what they came for, they leave; they see no point in staying any longer. This shows that they were not working for a disinterested idea: they were working for themselves. And those who come here for my sake, because they find me interesting or likeable, are no better off! There is no guarantee that, one day, they will not find me quite so much to their liking and will not leave me. I much prefer them to come for the Teaching, for the philosophy. Then we can be sure that they are here neither for themselves, nor for me or anyone else, but solely in order to work for the idea of the Universal White Brotherhood, to work to strengthen and nurture this idea and propagate it throughout mankind.

Some of the brothers and sisters come to the meetings of the Brotherhood only when I am there, and this proves that they cannot be counted on. Don't think that I am flattered by their attitude: I am not! If you believe that I am delighted when people come here for my sake, you are very mistaken! One day Mullah Nashrudin[3] went to the village cafe and, as he had come directly from his work, he was wearing his dirty, old, patched working clothes. Nobody took any notice of him. Nobody said, 'Hey, Mullah Nashrudin, come and join us. Have a cup of coffee! Have a piece of Turkish Delight!' Nobody even noticed him and he was very unhappy. So he went home and put on his smartest clothes, his great coat and his fur bonnet, and went back to the cafe. As soon as he entered, people took notice of him in his fine clothes: 'Hello, Mullah Nashrudin. Come and sit down. How are you? Have a cup of coffee! Have some Turkish Delight!' And Mullah Nashrudin, seeing all this, held up the

---

[3] Mullah Nashrudin, the name of a popular figure of fun in Turkish folklore.

skirt of his coat and spoke to it: Look at all that. It's all for you. Here, eat! Drink!' What a slap in the face for all those people. He showed them that he knew they had only welcomed him so warmly because of his fine clothes.

And, for me, the situation is exactly the same. People think that it gives me pleasure when they come here for me. Not at all; remember Mullah Nashrudin! The brothers and sisters don't realize that the 'me' they come for is nothing more than an overcoat. The real 'me' is not the one you see here, before you: the real 'me', my true self, is the Teaching. Yes, for I am welded to the Teaching; I have melted into it and identified with it. If you want to love me, love the Teaching and you will be loving me. You don't know who I am. Some of the brothers and sisters tell me, 'I can feel your presence in the wind. I feel you in the trees.' Yes, I am everywhere, in the whole of nature. The body that you see here, before you, is no more than a millionth part of what I really am. The rest of me is somewhere else!

Those who work for an idea are strong, powerful and reliable. Yes, and Heaven relies on them. As for the others, they are here one day and gone the next and they will never really understand anything. Our Teaching is divine, and we must work for it without asking to be rewarded. Whatever work you have been asked to do here, remember that you are doing it for the sake of the Teaching, for the sake of this one idea: that the Kingdom of God may be established on earth, that harmony and love be disseminated throughout the world. If you do this, even your health problems will disappear. Yes, and this is why I can say that the only true doctors, the only true healers on earth are Initiates, because they go to the roots of illness. Others intervene when it is already too late. Human beings should be cared for before they fall ill. As soon as disharmony (hatred, scandal-mongering, viciousness, envy and revolt) begins to eat into them, illness has begun. For illness is disorder. And what can you expect? When one kind of disorder meets another kind of disorder, they get along very well together! Whereas if harmony

Harmony

dwells within you, disorder cannot get in; your inner harmony stands in the way. These are very important laws which you must know.

If you are really concerned about your own evolution, about final victory, you must work for harmony: work to harmonize your whole being with the forces of the universe. The power of a disciple resides, precisely, in his will to be in harmony: if this is what he really wants, no one can stop him from achieving it. He possesses the free will to vibrate in harmony with the body of the universe, to climb to the highest peak and live with the life of God Himself.

For the whole universe is nothing but harmony, the universal harmony which is known as the Music of the Spheres and which I once had the privilege of hearing. It was an indescribable experience, the sensation of being drawn out of myself and stretched to the limits of space made it almost unbearable. Yes, Heaven gave me the privilege of hearing the Music of the Spheres.

It is not difficult to know whether or not you have succeeded in achieving harmony: your whole being will tell you. When all your cells vibrate together in unison you cannot fail to feel it. If, when you are thirsty, you drink a glass of water, you don't need anyone to tell you that your thirst is quenched, do you? Similarly, when you have attained a state of harmony, you don't need to be told: you feel the influx of tremendous forces, your aura pulses and vibrates, you are in a state of wonder and delight. And if, on the contrary, you are in a state of disorder and chaos, do you need to be told what a piteous state you are in? No, you know it already. In fact, if someone were to come and praise you when you were feeling like that, you would be so embarrassed you would want to disappear under the ground!

You see, the Invisible World teaches each one of us, without exception, by means of experience. But the trouble is that human beings do not understand this language, so they do not draw any conclusions from their experiences. And yet this is where your real work lies: in reflecting on your experiences and in drawing the right conclusions from them; this is what will enable you to make much more rapid progress and go much further on the path of spirituality. But do you do this? No, you repeat the same disastrous experiences all your lives long, and never do anything to remedy the situation. You suffer from the situation, to be sure; you are not very proud of yourselves, to be sure, but you are so used to the prevalent disorder that you never react or attempt to change it. Everybody just flounders along in the same old rut. My dear brothers and sisters: hurry up and understand that you must drag yourselves out of that rut! And the best way to do this is to meditate on harmony; wish for harmony, yearn for harmony, love harmony. Introduce it into everything you do, into every movement, every word, every look. It is not so terribly difficult, after all! You should have been doing this for years now; ever since you started coming here, you should have been working only on harmony. But you all choose just one modest little quality or virtue to cultivate: patience, tolerance, generosity, etc. Oh, they are all right, I admit; but they are only scraps compared to the immensity of collective harmony. Obviously, it is excellent to be generous, kind, indulgent, gentle and humble; but there are a lot of people who still live in disharmony in spite of all these virtues; they are not enough to make them perfect. So you would do better to leave them alone; don't bother about them any more! You are horrified, aren't you? 'But that's a terrible thing to say! How can you give such bad advice? Religion has never taught anything like that!' No, but you would do much better to leave religion alone, too! Take care of this one thing: harmony, and it will take care of all the other virtues.

When you have managed to touch someone's heart, you have touched his whole being. If you touch only his feet, or a finger or an ear, it will not have much effect. But touch his heart, and his whole being will begin to feel involved. If you have been deeply moved by someone, you say, 'He spoke to my heart'. So we have to reach the heart: the heart of other beings, the heart of things, the heart of the universe. And you can only reach the heart of the universe by means of harmony. Thanks to harmony you will attract all the other virtues and qualities; they will flock to you because you have touched the heart and not just the outskirts, the fringe.

Ah, if you want to touch the heart of the universe you will never do so with your ten-a-penny qualities. It does not make much difference whether you are avaricious or generous, irritable or peaceful, compassionate or hard-hearted. There are many very virtuous people who have never succeeded in touching the heart of the Eternal Father. You can only touch His heart by being in harmony with Him, by vibrating in unison with Him, in other words, by submitting to Him and doing His will. And it is in this context that the word 'submission' becomes crucial. If you refuse to submit to the authority of ignorant, evil human beings you are not sinning against the Eternal One, because you have no obligation to be in unison with all the imbeciles and malefactors in the world. But you do have the obligation to obey Almighty God, and if you do this, your own reason will tell you whether or not to obey human beings. In wanting to be independent and free from the Lord, human beings oppose His will and put obstacles in the way of His plans. In this way they repeat the sin of Lucifer and our first parents. This desire to liberate oneself, to be anarchic, to defy God's orders, is the cause of all the misfortunes of mankind. This is something you simply must understand. For my part, I understand it in all its magnitude and it is very simple, very clear, very easy to express in a few words: the day men broke the bonds that were their link with Heavenly harmony, misfortune began to rain down on them. And things are bound to go on getting worse, for men are moving ceaselessly further and further from God, becoming more and more lawless and anarchic; they have no respect for anything any more. Yes, all this is reaching terrifying proportions. Wherever you look, even those who follow a religion or a spiritual teaching... everyone is contaminated by the germs of anarchy; we had better get used to the idea of catastrophic events to come.

Even in a Teaching like ours, capable though it is of bringing all human beings, all hearts and souls, together in this luminous understanding, there are many who are not really willing to understand. They prefer to open their minds and hearts to the prevailing currents of anarchy, rather than working for universal harmony. This is why I cannot be perfectly happy. Not that it changes anything for me, personally, of course: I attained this inner harmony a long time ago. But my happiness cannot be complete yet, because the goal of my happiness is your happiness and that of all men. As far as my own responsibility goes, I have done the work I had to do, I have attained harmony with the Deity; I enjoy absolute happiness and fulfilment. But that is not the end of my task: my task is not to be like so many religious people whose only ambition was to save their own souls. My task is to do everything in my power to help others to achieve what I have achieved. But I am not succeeding. I try to lead them forward, to drag them after me, but they don't understand; they don't follow. This is why I cannot be completely happy: I have not been given the task of being happy all by myself, but of getting every human being to share this happiness.

If you would only make the effort to understand these truths in greater depth, you would enjoy the same conceptions, the same light, the same plenitude that I enjoy, then I would be supported and helped and, together, we could revolutionize the world and do good to every single human being. But a great many of you cannot follow me because they don't want to understand; I can feel it. Their minds are occupied by all kinds of other things that are opposed to what I tell you. Is there any wonder that this saddens me? I repeat: it is not for myself that I am saddened. I have already resolved a great many problems of my own. But my work is not to find happiness in doing the will of Heaven all alone!

So, you see, my dear brothers and sisters, since Heaven has sent you here to be 'tormented' by me, there is only one thing for you to do, and that is to work for harmony. Instead of wasting your time thinking about all kinds of other things: your favourite amusements, your business deals, your latest love affair, think about harmony. Think about achieving harmony within your whole being, so that all your cells vibrate in unison. Take the example of an orchestra: everyone has heard orchestral concerts and knows that it takes only one player playing out of tune to destroy the harmony of the whole orchestra. And the same is true of our physical bodies, our whole beings, in which our organs are the instruments of an orchestra: they have to play together. Try to read when you have a splitting headache, diarrhoea or toothache: the disharmony within you prevents you from taking in what you are reading. But, once the pain has eased and things are beginning to function properly again, you have no trouble understanding. You could find quantities of examples in your everyday lives to help you to understand the importance of harmony! An orchestra, a choir, a ballet, even a military parade: they all have to be harmonious. Everything in nature and in our own lives bears this lesson of harmony, order and beauty, but men continue to live in inner disorder and tumult! Ah, human beings... what a rebellious lot they are! They can never agree to harmonize themselves with the laws of the universe. In fact, human beings are the only ones who behave like that: animals, insects and plants, the spirits of nature, the Angels... They are all in harmony except men! Yes, men are anarchists!

So, now, put everything else to one side and think about harmony: nothing else. Harmonize yourselves with the whole of creation. And, in a flash, as soon as you reach a state of true harmony, you will understand all the laws of the universe, for harmony makes it possible to embrace everything in one glance.

The Bonfin, 15 July 1970

II

Whatever other faculties and powers you may possess, you will never be fully successful if you have not learned to be inwardly harmonious.

Take the example of a magus who is preparing to perform a magic rite: he puts on his ceremonial robes and, with the sword or wand in his hand, he steps into the magic circle that he has just drawn. But if harmony does not reign within him, not only will he not achieve the results he hoped for, but he will be in considerable danger. He may be extremely powerful, but the spirits will not do his will if there is no harmony within him. The greatest magi know this very well: they would never attempt to perform a magic rite without being in perfect communion with Heaven and the whole universe. A great many sorcerers and magicians, however, think that it is enough to know the formulas in order to get results. In fact, they could not be more wrong; they are laying themselves open to attack from every kind of malevolent entity. Nothing can be truly efficacious until one has achieved inner peace, and this goes far beyond the question of magic. So many of the things you do are done in disharmony! You kiss your wife and children or your friends when you are feeling sad, worried or remorseful. Even your most important tasks are undertaken in an attitude of disharmony: no wonder they are so rarely successful!

Every morning, when you first wake up, you should begin the day by attuning yourself to the world of universal harmony. Only then should you get your breakfast, talk to your children, kiss them and get them dressed, or go to work. When you go to visit someone, your first thought on entering their house should be: 'May peace and harmony reign in this house!' But don't delude yourselves: there are not many who think of doing this. They go in, and before you know it, they have sown discord between husband and wife or parents and children! And when you look at people in the street or shops, everywhere, even in schools, all one sees is their lack of harmony. How can teachers possibly teach their pupils in such conditions?

The laws of harmony are the most solemn laws of the universe. Think about this, meditate and observe yourself and your reactions and see what state you are in when you act; then you will understand why, in certain cases, you fail to get good results. Even when your intention is to do good, if you yourself are not in harmony, the good you hope for will not have the conditions it needs to manifest itself; in fact you will be disturbing something in the invisible world. You must never undertake anything when you are in disharmony, and this applies, above all, to the creation of children! Parents should be extremely vigilant on this point: if they do not unite in harmony to create a child, they will have cause to regret it for the rest of their lives, for Hell itself will enter into that child. People are willing to spend days and months preparing themselves and trying to obtain everything else in life, but one minute of their time is too much to spend on harmonizing themselves: they think that they are already prepared.

Harmony is the corner-stone of all success, of every divine realization. It must be your constant preoccupation to introduce harmony into your being; only on this condition can you begin to accomplish certain tasks which will bear fruit for eternity. A tremendous amount of work, and tremendous strength of mind and concentration are needed to achieve this harmony! But once one has achieved it, prodigious forces are at one's command for the good of mankind. Can't you feel that the whole universe, all the forces of nature, agree with what I am saying? Just take a good, hard look and you will see that the whole of nature confirms and endorses my words.

A world of harmony exists, an eternal world from which have come all forms, colours, sounds, perfumes and flavours. Yes, and I have been in that world; years ago, Heaven gave me the privilege of tasting this perfect harmony: I was snatched from my body and permitted to hear the Harmony of the Spheres. Never since, have I experienced anything to equal it in intensity and richness. There is nothing that I can compare it to. It was so beautiful, so divine that I was afraid; I was afraid of that splendour, for I felt my whole being expanding to such an extent that I was in danger of dissolving and disintegrating into space. So I cut short the ecstasy and came back to earth. Now, I regret it, of course! But at least, for a few seconds, I actually experienced, I actually saw and heard how the whole universe vibrated. Rocks, trees, mountains, the oceans and stars, the suns and every creature, sang together in such magnificent, sublime harmony, it was as though... But, no! It cannot be compared to anything that can be heard in the physical world. And I was afraid! Yes, it was so powerful, so intense, only a few seconds more and I would have disintegrated. Heaven gave me that experience so that I should have some idea of what Heavenly harmony really is. Pythagoras and Plato and many other philosophers have talked about this harmony, but I wonder how many of them actually experienced it.

And now, the memory of that experience is enough to fill my soul, as though nothing else were needed to sustain, strengthen and nourish my spiritual life. Yes, it is enough to know how the universe is put together; to know how it all vibrates in harmony, in accordance with the will of Cosmic Intelligence from whom every object and every living being has received its own particular note, its own voice. Unfortunately, we cannot hear how the Creator has accorded and harmonized all His creatures. But I only have to think of this to find myself in a state that defies description. Believe me, I am not deceiving you; Heaven hears what I am saying and I know what a grave fault it would be to lie before Heaven. Before the Eternal One, therefore, before all the sublime Intelligences above, I tell you this: I have heard the Music of the Spheres. You can believe me or not, as you please – it makes no difference to me – but I consider this to be the rarest privilege that any human being can receive.

For those of you who would like to explore this question further, let me say a little about harmony from the Cabbalistic point of view. Each Sephirah of the Tree of Life, which I have already spoken about, expresses a particular nuance of the divine harmony, but the Sephirah that presides over the Harmony of the Spheres is Chokmah, and the name of God in this Sephirah is Yah. His servant is Raziel, Archangel of light, knowledge and wisdom and of the power of the Divine Word. Raziel commands the Ophanim (the Cherubim of the Christian religion) who, under the authority of the Word, watch over the harmony of the cosmos. Their empire is immense, stretching all the way to the Zodiac, known in Hebrew as Mazloth.

I have often heard people expressing astonishment at the unity that characterizes all the lectures I have given you over the years; it is as though everything I said flowed from one central source, for nothing I say ever contradicts what I have said before. Yes, and let me tell you that it is not because of all the books I have read that I am able to see this unity so clearly, it is because I have heard the Music of the Spheres. In the presence of that harmony one understands the structure and destination of the universe and how it lives and vibrates. People believe that one has to read books to learn the secrets of creation, that it takes long years of study to discover truth. No, if you want to know the universe you have to learn to vibrate in unison with it, thanks to your organs of spiritual knowledge: the solar plexus, the Hara chakra and the aura.

For years, I practised astral projection and went out of my physical body to study that marvellous construction, that organization that we call the cosmos. In this way I was able to contemplate the universe, not as we see it with our eyes, clothed in flesh and blood, but as a structure in the world of archetypes. To hear the Harmony of the Spheres was the crowning point of all my research, all my work, all my out-of-body experiences. And, ever since, it has remained as a criterion, an example, a touchstone, a model which enables me to understand and evaluate everything else.

I realize that I may be making these revelations a little prematurely. A lot of people have already said to me, 'You don't realize what you are saying! You're centuries ahead of your times! Nobody is capable of applying what you teach. Who is going to follow you?' Yes, I know that. But even if no one is ready to follow me, I am telling you these things because that is what I have been ordered to do. Besides, as everything I say is taken down in shorthand or recorded, one day there will come a new race of men with a different structure and a different intelligence, and they will be capable of following and applying this Teaching. At the moment it is not possible: I know that. Human beings are not yet capable of putting such tremendous truths into practice in their lives. But that does not matter; I still have to talk about them. I must make them known, so that the few who are capable of doing so have the possibility of following this path. My job is to do the work I am asked to do; that's all!

All those who are not interested in learning the essential truths of this Teaching can go somewhere else. I shall certainly not hold them back for, to tell the truth, they are no use to us, here. Yes, my dear brothers and sisters, like Stradivarius, I make violins, but I cannot make them out of just any kind of wood and varnish. The violins I am making must be so sensitive and also so strong that Heaven can make its own music on them;

otherwise I should be wasting my time. Everyone has a goal in life, and my goal is not to bring crowds and crowds of people here, but to train workers for the Kingdom of God. Yes, I need workers, and if I do not manage to create real workers, real violinists, true servants of God, I shall have wasted my time and worked for nothing. Which one of you ever tries to see things from my point of view? If only you would sometimes say to yourselves: 'The Master is there to help us, to enlighten and instruct us and put us in touch with Heaven; but isn't there something that we should be doing for him? Doesn't he have a desire, a wish that we could do something about?' Yes, if you thought about it like that, you would soon discover that there is something that I want also. And it is not something for myself; that is the great difference. I want all those who come here to be animated by a single ideal: the ideal of spreading light. Nobody tries to put themselves in my place and understand what I want.

I am not complaining; I am simply asking you to try to see things from my point of view and to understand that I want workers, true servants of God. I am working for the whole world and if you do not want to help me by working for my ideas as I am working for you, it is unjust. There is a Law of Justice in the world, according to which he who takes must also give; only he who gives has the right to take. Justice is a fair exchange, a mutual giving and receiving. But if you take, without giving anything in exchange, you are committing an injustice, and the laws of Karma will be set in motion and come and make their claims on you. No one has the slightest notion of the value of just one of my lectures. In your opinion, perhaps, they are not worth much, but in the opinion of Heaven they are so precious that no one in the whole world can ever have enough money to pay what they are worth. In fact, that is why those who come and listen to them are never asked to pay.

Well, from now on you know that I draw everything I tell you in my lectures from the region in which I heard the

Heavenly Harmony, the Music of the Spheres. In fact it is this Music that explains everything to me, although, if the truth be told there is not really so much that needs to be explained. All one has to do is to achieve this harmony and, in an instant, everything becomes clear and one understands God's wisdom, one understands peace, one understands love. Time and again I have heard you say, 'Yesterday I understood everything! Why do I understand nothing today?' The answer is that you have disrupted your inner harmony. This is why I tell you: 'Soak yourselves in the word "harmony", night and day. Think of nothing else. Keep it in your mind as a tuning-fork, and as soon as you feel that you are slightly upset or off-balance, listen to it and tune your whole being to it.'

The Bonfin, 27 August 1970

III

'Immerse yourself in silence. Abandon yourself to the embrace of silence as a child abandons itself to the embrace of its mother's arms, and harmony will grow within you and reach into every smallest cell of your body.'

I don't think this text needs any explanation; it is very clear. You only have to remember what I have already told you about harmony: if you work to bring harmony into yourself, to live it and spread it round you, there will be no need for you to work at developing each particular virtue or quality. There, this is the first time I have told you that you should not try to develop a particular virtue, and I say this because it is a very time-consuming method! A whole life a time would probably not be enough, and, while you are working at one virtue, what would you do about all the others? Your whole life would be spent in becoming patient, or tolerant or gentle, and all the other qualities would be neglected.

So, I repeat: don't focus on this or that virtue in particular. Concentrate only on harmony and, at one stroke, it will cause all the other virtues to flower as well. This is what I do; I leave all the other virtues alone. I make no attempt to become generous or patient or indulgent; it is simply not worthwhile; it would be a waste of time. I am interested only in living in harmony and I have seen for myself that this enables me to manifest all the other virtues as well, for harmony forces me to be intelligent and wise and understanding. Just try being wise or kind when your inner life is in turmoil: you will not succeed! And the reason is simply your appalling state of inner confusion and disharmony. This is a question you should think seriously about. Harmonize everything within you and you will find that you are capable of such wisdom, perspicacity and intelligence that you will astonish yourself and wonder where it all came from! Yes, if you are guided by harmony you will be capable of untangling all kinds of difficult situations and helping others by finding solutions and giving good advice. Shun disharmony as your worst enemy for, once it gets a grip on you, it will ravage and destroy you and there is no virtue capable of saving you.

Harmony, you see, is the synthesis of all qualities and every virtue. When you cultivate harmony you touch the heart of reality, the Universal Soul, the Centre. And from this central core come the orders and the currents and forces that transform and organize everything. When you are not in a state of harmony, when you are upset, irritable or tense, you may make heroic efforts to manifest at least one virtue, but it will be to no avail. All that is bad and destructive in you rises to the surface to bite and sting and kick and destroy. However hard you try you will never make much progress, because you have forgotten the mother of all qualities and virtues: harmony. When you are in a state of harmony, everything in you blossoms: the expression of your eyes and face are more beautiful, your gestures are measured and more graceful, your words more constructive, your thoughts more intelligent. It is said that sloth is the mother of all vices; but nobody ever speaks of the mother of all virtues which is harmony.

Musicians, of course, can talk about harmony; in fact you would be astonished at the wealth of their explanations. But they cannot reveal the Initiatic aspect of harmony to you, because they don't know it themselves. From a strictly musical point of view, they have a lot to teach, but no musician is capable of telling you the things I have just told you about harmony: the fact that harmony is related to every virtue, to perfection and even to health. Yes, above all to health, for the least sign of disharmony undermines and erodes one's health. He who understands this will have only one desire: to attune himself to the Entities and Intelligences of the divine world, to create harmony within every cell of his being.

Only harmony can flood us with the precious blessings and gifts of Heaven, for Heaven responds only to the voice of harmony. If you want to talk to Heaven, to beg for a favour or for protection, you must realize that there is no other language. You can rant and rave (and even threaten never to go church again if you don't get what you want!), but it will make no difference: Heaven will remain unmoved. But if you speak the language of music, by which I mean the language of harmony which is absolute music, music itself, music *par excellence*, then Heaven will hear you and answer your prayer. There is only one language spoken in Heaven, the language of harmony, and if you are capable of speaking to Heaven in that language, it will respond by sending you everything in abundance.

I see you spending a great deal of effort in the pursuit of many different things, in the belief that they are more important than harmony. You think that they will shelter and protect you and bring you happiness and, in the meantime, you neglect harmony. But perhaps you will understand me better today for, as I have pointed out, it is in your own interest. It is very much to your advantage to work ceaselessly and untiringly for harmony, for it is the only thing that can give you all the other things you long for: friendship, love and, above all, the Divine Presence. It has often happened already that, when we have been singing together, our singing has brought us closer to perfect harmony and you have felt the presence of heavenly entities amongst us. This is what attracts them: the harmony. They come amongst us, distributing flowers and other gifts, and you sense their presence, but without realizing what it is you are feeling. Continue to make every effort, to do everything in your power to create harmony until Heaven yields and comes amongst us; and I assure you, it will come. It is already with us, It is behind all our efforts and, one day, you will witness marvellous manifestations. When that day comes you will be filled with such joy that you will be unable to contain it all. You will be flooded by currents so powerful that you will throb and vibrate in purest ecstasy.

I repeat: harmony is the most effective weapon you can have against illness. If you are ill it means that there is some form of disorder within you; you have harboured certain negative thoughts, feelings or attitudes and they are reflected in your health. Why are they reflected in one organ rather than in another? Because it has all been calculated with mathematical precision, depending upon which law you have broken. If you want to be cured, you must think of nothing but harmony: day and night you must endeavour to conform, to be synchronized, to accord and align yourself with Life, with limitless, cosmic Life. For this is what true harmony is. It is not enough to be in harmony with a few individuals: your husband or wife, your children, parents, neighbours and friends. You must be in harmony with Universal Life. Unfortunately, many people are in perfect accord with a few mediocre individuals and completely out of tune with Universal Life! Little by little that lack of harmony filters into every nook and cranny of their being and takes possession of them and then, one day, it shows up in the form of illness.

Don't think that I exclude myself from any of this. Not at all, I tell myself all that I am telling you. If I am ill or have a pain, I tell myself, 'You see? This shows that you still haven't attained the harmony that you are always talking about to the brothers and sisters. So get to work!' I am just as much concerned by what I am talking about, as you are. You will probably say, 'In that case, you are not so tremendously advanced or highly evolved, either.' You are right, I am not so tremendously advanced! But the essential difference between myself and a great many others is that I understand the importance of harmony, whereas the others have still not understood. Certainly, there are still many things in me that need to be cleansed, purified, transformed, sublimated, vivified and resuscitated. Don't imagine that I was perfect when I came into the world! Even Initiates inherit flaws and failings. When they reincarnate they have to accept to be born into families from which they inevitably inherit imperfections and illness. Yes, but then they work overtime: twice, three times, a hundred times harder than others, to accelerate the process of cleansing and purification. This explains how they manage to attain a state of harmony much more rapidly than others. That's all. You must not be so naïve as to believe that when an Initiate is born, everything within him is absolutely pure, harmonious and divine! I know better: in reality it is not like that at all! But that is not really the point: you must never excuse yourself on the grounds that you have inherited this or that failing from your parents. Instead, you should simply say, 'If I had deserved better, I would have been sent to reincarnate in a better family. It's not my parents' fault; it's my own. So now it is up to me to tidy everything up, and clean and purify myself.' And then, after a while, you will be rejuvenated, luminous and radiant. To be sure, though, you have to be very strong-minded and very much aware... and you have to take it seriously.

From now on, leave everything else to one side and concern yourself only with harmony! It is harmony that will bring with it all the other things you need: health, beauty, light, joy and the most extraordinary sense of blessedness; you will feel so strong and unassailable that even death will hold no fears for you. Yes, thanks to harmony you will conquer death. But, of course, there is one thing you have to remember, and that is that in order to create harmony you have to love it. As long as you don't truly love harmony you will never persuade it to come to you. But I can feel that you are beginning to love it. For quite some time now, you have been making a sincere effort to create harmony in the Brotherhood. You are doing this consciously and powerfully and you have already seen some inexpressibly beautiful results. Continue to create harmony and, one day, I will reveal to you all the transformations that are taking place throughout the world because of the work we are doing here. In countless families in many countries all over the world, men and women who long to free themselves from the disorder that reigns in today's world, are receiving inspiration thanks to our work and the mere fact of our existence here, in the Universal White Brotherhood.

This, too, is something that escapes you: you cannot really see why we must live in harmony. It is because, by doing so, we ourselves begin to taste the reality of the Kingdom of God and, above all, because by doing so we are projecting into the world, and even to the stars in the heavens, currents, waves and forces of such power and splendour that, sooner or later, the whole of mankind will be obliged to improve and transform itself and live in harmony, happiness and peace.

The Bonfin, 10 August 1971

Chapter Two

MEDICAL SCIENCE MUST BE BASED ON INITIATIC SCIENCE

I have greetings and all kinds of good wishes for you from all those who are at the Bonfin! Yes, my dear brothers and sisters, an immense crowd of people – How many? Oh, about ten or twelve – but they all send you their love. Some of them will be coming to join us here, so you might wonder why they sent you messages in advance? Well, it always gives one pleasure to be remembered, doesn't it?

There was once a Bulgarian who returned to Sofia after visiting the authorities of the Orthodox Church in Istanbul. 'What news have you brought for us?' asked a priest. 'Aha,' said the man; 'I heard that they were thinking of making you a bishop or an archimandrate.' 'What nonsense', replied the priest; 'You're pulling my leg!' But a few days later, the two men met again, and the priest said, 'So, at least they know that I exist, do they? Tell me what they said about me.' You see, that is how human beings are: the priest wanted to appear humble, but he was secretly delighted to learn that people in high places were talking about him!

If we could only look inside each one of us, what a lot of extraordinary things we would find! Actually, it is not even necessary to look. We know human nature, and we know what we would find. You will probably say, 'Lord, how negative he is!' No, I am not being negative, I meant that we would also find some magnificent, divine things. The trouble is, you never let me finish, so, of course, you misunderstand me; you might at least let me finish what I am saying!

But seriously, there are some very good things to be found in human beings, on condition that you pass through certain dense, dark regions very quickly, and go directly to the luminous, subtle regions in the highest part of their being. If you do this, you will find that what I say is true: you will be dazzled by the splendour you find there. Take anyone at all: if you look no further than the outside, you will not see anything very impressive. In fact, it is sometimes frightful! But if you try to see what exists on a higher level you will always find another nature. True, it may still be dormant, but it is there, all the same, waiting for the right moment to manifest itself. If that other nature could be aroused and if, at the same time, you could hold back certain negative manifestations, you would see an extraordinary transformation. For every human being possesses both a higher and a lower nature within him.

But I did not come here to talk to you about that. As a matter of fact, as usual, I came without knowing what I was going to talk about. Usually, as soon as I have given you the greetings I have been asked to pass on to you, my one idea is to make myself scarce. But once I am with you it is not so easy to get away again in a hurry! Yes, I have noticed that: once I am with you I cannot tear myself away. I can feel that you are all thinking, 'Talk to us about something!' But I really mean it: I don't know what to tell you. Why don't we just go our separate ways until Christmas Day? No? You really want me to continue? Tell me honestly: aren't you tired? Well, I only have to look at you: I must admit that I cannot see a single face that looks sleepy or tired. How wonderful to see so many faces alight with energy!

Don't you think it is wonderful to go on talking without saying anything? I often do it, don't I? Except, of course, when I am simmering with indignation; when that happens I say all kinds of sensible things. Sensible from my point of view, anyway: perhaps others don't find them so sensible! But when I am perfectly calm I can find nothing to say. There was a sister, once (I have often mentioned her to you, and now she has gone to the next world: may the Lord give her light and peace!), who often rendered me service: she was always grumbling and criticizing and upsetting the Brotherhood, so that I was obliged to keep rectifying things. Oh yes, she kept me very busy, I can tell you! But thanks to her I gave much better lectures! Now, don't take that to mean that you should start doing what she did, just to supply me with material for my lectures! On the contrary, for the truth is that it is harmony that inspires me with the best topics. Often, when we are meditating together and you are all concentrating on light, it is as though a bouquet of sparks rose like a fountain over your heads, and this creates a marvellous state of mind in me and inspires me to talk to you.

As a matter of fact, the beneficial effects of harmony on human health is being increasingly acknowledged: it is becoming more and more evident that many illnesses are caused by a long standing condition of inner disharmony: disharmony in people's thoughts and feelings. Doctors have all kinds of scientific names for these illnesses, whereas I continue to refer to them in the simplest terms which are self-explanatory, and my name for all these illnesses is 'disharmony'. If you observe the effects of harmony and disharmony in every domain, in every activity and every area of society, whatever scientific label you choose to give them, it always boils down to a question of harmony or disharmony, order or disorder. Yes, modern medicine has found cures for the plague, cholera and typhus, for instance, but it has still not found cures for the nervous disorders human beings suffer from: anxiety, phobias, nervous collapse or depression, which, in turn, have an extremely debilitating effect on the physical organism. And, as you know, illnesses change and move from one part of the body to another: in the past, certain parts of the body seemed to be more affected by illness and, nowadays, other parts are more frequently affected: the nervous system or the heart, for instance. The illnesses themselves have changed also, of course, and though they are not always incurable, many of them are very widespread and some, such as poliomyelitis or cancer are extremely difficult to cure.

I am very glad to see signs that the medical professions are beginning to change some of their positions, and that entirely new trends, closer to the truths of our Teaching, are becoming more and more apparent. As the explanations and points of view exposed in our Teaching are all part of the Initiatic Science that traces its origins to the earliest days of mankind, it shows that conventional medical science is gradually turning back to the great truths of the past. Recently, doctors have been somewhat disturbed by the frequent reactions against treatment with antibiotics and chemotherapy, which have sometimes had very negative effects. Some are beginning to turn to homoeopathy[1] because they realize that allopathic medicine treats the disease rather than the patient; it forgets about the whole person with all his individual, specific characteristics. They have also seen that treatments which effectively destroy the harmful microbes or viruses that cause illness, often destroy useful micro-organisms at the same time.

Medical science is also beginning to realize that man's psychic faculties set him apart from all the other categories of living beings. Doctors recognize that the same drug does not always have the same effect on different patients, which means that they cannot necessarily treat different patients suffering from the same illness with the same remedies. Good homoeopathic doctors study each individual patient in detail;

---

[1] This lecture was given in 1967.

they take into account his temperament and psychic situation and even his likes and dislikes, and then they prescribe a remedy that is suited to him, but which may be quite unsuited to someone else. They know that each patient must be seen within the framework of all the circumstances and elements which make up the 'terrain' or breeding ground of disease, whereas orthodox medicine, in concentrating on the illness itself, has neglected the circumstances leading to its development.

Another recent trend is a revival of interest in the principles taught by Hippocrates. Hippocrates was a Greek doctor who had studied the medical science of Egypt and India, and who taught that the most important thing was to help the body to defend itself against disease, for the organism – that is to say, nature – has its own defence mechanisms. When attacked by agents of disease, the body spontaneously manufactures chemical elements that effectively neutralize the invader, whereas if this defence mechanism has been undermined by all kinds of drugs, the body cannot react as it should. Hippocrates used natural means to increase the resistance to disease: baths, herbal infusions, sunbathing, rest, purification and fasting, etc. But today sick people take so many drugs that they actually weaken their natural resistance and prevent their body from defending itself; in relying so heavily on external means of defence, they fail to develop and reinforce their own innate strength. And this applies to you, also: be careful! Don't swallow anything and everything, otherwise your organism will soon be unable to defend itself against attack. A great many anomalies are due to the abuse of pharmaceutical products.

So, as I say, some elements of the medical establishment are turning back to Hippocrates, to nature. For example, they are beginning to recognize the merits of sea water, and one sees more and more centres for thalassotherapy. Sea water contains all the materials needed by the body: exactly those elements that are to be found in our blood. The Egyptian doctors who cured

Plato did so with thalassotherapy, and the ancient Babylonians, Chinese and Japanese practised this type of therapy. I very much agree with these kinds of medicine, for they correspond to our Teaching which wants to help man to restore his inner balance by drawing all the elements his body needs from the inexhaustible reservoirs of nature. The latest scientific discoveries confirm that man's body contains all the elements contained in the oceans, for, like all other living creatures, human beings came originally from the sea. When he is immersed once again in his primordial element, the sea, man is restored to his original equilibrium.

It is also very good to drink sea water, and one way to do this is by eating oysters. You will ask, 'But can't you find the same elements in pills produced in laboratories?' No, it is not the same thing; the elements you get from the sea are alive, and your organism absorbs and assimilates them differently. I cannot really recommend any of the numerous products that men manufacture in their factories and laboratories. Some people claim that all the minerals found in sea water come from the rain and the rivers and spring waters that have filtered through the soil, but the latest research shows that iodine, boron and other very rare elements found in the sea, are not found on dry land: it is still not known where they come from.

As a matter of fact, I have plans to use sea water, one day, at the Bonfin: we can transport it by tanker and heat it for hot baths, for, as recent scientific research has shown, when it is heated it enters the blood stream. And we can add seaweed to the water, for it also has remarkable therapeutic properties. My grandmother used to cure people this way, so I have known for more than sixty years that it is possible to restore harmony in one's organism by the use of hot baths of sea water and seaweed. But it is also good to eat seaweed. The Japanese owe their remarkable powers of resistance to the fact that they eat a lot of seaweed. When I visited the Hawaiian Islands I saw shops that sold all kinds of fish and shellfish, and also several different kinds of seaweed; I have never seen or tasted anything of quite the same shape, consistency and flavour anywhere else. And people bought quantities of these seaweeds. Ah, if we could only get them here! They contain all the nutrients we need. Of course, you can buy them in specialized food shops, but you have to be wary of what you are buying, for they are not always fresh, and you never know how they have been prepared. It would be so much better to go and collect them from the right places yourselves, but it is not easy, the seas are so polluted!

But you can see what people are like, can't you? Those who recommend thalassotherapy are enthusiastic about the benefits of sea water and seaweed, but they never pause to wonder where the forces and energies transmitted by the sea come from. They always forget the one, essential factor: the sun! It is the sun that gives sea water and seaweed the vitality that human beings benefit from. It is the sun that is the vital factor: the water and plants are simply mediums, transmitters. If the sea were not vivified by the sun it would have nothing beneficial to offer.

Human reasoning always misses the essence of a situation because men do not possess true knowledge: it never occurs to them that it is the sun that gives them everything that they find on earth. Take a tree, for example: what is a tree? Nothing more nor less than a reservoir of condensed sunlight. When you burn a tree, all that condensed light goes back to the sun, leaving behind it only a small quantity of gas, water vapour and earth in the form of ashes. And the oceans, like a tree, are simply reservoirs of sunlight. The sun looks at the sea and pours its own life into it, then, when we drink its water or bathe in it, we, in turn, receive this life that the sea has received from the sun.

Phytotherapy and aromatherapy, both of which use plants, are also excellent therapeutic methods, for plants also have the property of receiving and condensing elements from the sun and stars; I have great confidence in their therapeutic virtues. If you know the right doses to use and how to combine them, they have no adverse side effects. So I advise you to use plants as much as possible; in fact I would like to set aside some land at the Bonfin for the cultivation of the most useful aromatic plants. I would indicate the properties of each plant and you could all take away a supply when you go home.

Yet another form of therapy that I recommend is the very ancient science of chiropractic, which was rediscovered by an American and has gradually spread to all the other countries. You may remember that I have often emphasized the importance of the spine, and told you that many illnesses are caused by a deviation of the spinal column or a pinched nerve, etc. Since the nerves supply different organs, it is no good trying to cure the organs if you do nothing to cure the nerves that supply them; and these nerves run through the spinal column. The spinal column acts as a bridge between the brain and the organs and the rest of the body and, if this bridge is not in good condition, it will inevitably cause anomalies in the organs. The normal functioning of the organs can be restored by taking care of the nerves that run through the spinal column. Those who have studied this science have cured many different illnesses, even deafness, for, in some cases, deafness is due to a defect in the spinal column.

Magnetism is yet another form of therapy; in fact magnetism and phytotherapy are two of the most ancient therapeutic methods known to man. From the beginning of time Initiates have used magnetism to heal people. The Gospels tell us that Jesus touched the sick and healed them. How? By instilling into them a force, his own force, a harmonious, perfect fluid. It was as though he had given them an injection of life. And what is the effect of life? Exactly the same as that of the pure air you breathe into your lungs, or of a blood transfusion: it sets the organism back on an even keel. When an Initiate touches someone who is ill, therefore, thanks to the fact that he himself lives a harmonious, fulfilled, divine life, he effects a veritable transfusion of vitality. It is as though he administered a transfusion of his own blood which immediately sets the sick person back on his feet. Yes, as I say, magnetism is the most ancient form of medicine; it is the medicine of the Initiates who healed with a touch, a glance or simply a word, without physical contact of any kind. Actually, it is a kind of injection, for it consists in 'injecting' something into the sick person's body.

There are many more different kinds of therapy. Before the war, already, some were interested in cellulotherapy. They cured and prolonged life or retarded the aging process by injecting into the human body a solution of cells taken from the glands, spleen, liver, kidneys, etc., of certain animals. This type of therapy has been known for centuries; in fact Paracelsus knew it. We all know that in Africa and America there are still tribes which have the custom of eating certain organs of animals in order to acquire the qualities of those animals. They believe, for instance, that if they eat the heart of a lion they will acquire the strength and courage of a lion, whereas if they eat the heart of a rabbit they will become timid and fearful. It is true that cellulotherapy can give good results, but it is a form of black magic, for it necessitates the sacrifice of living creatures. So this is one kind of therapy that I do not recommend. Serge Voronoff, for example, transplanted glands from monkeys into human beings in order to revive their flagging sexual activity, but the method was abandoned when it was found that although many people recovered their sexual energy by this method, they also reverted to animality. In any case, to take cells from animals and graft them into human beings is certainly not something I recommend; in spite of its efficacy, therefore, you must choose other methods.

I am obliged to reject whatever is incompatible with the Science that I have studied: Initiatic Science. Initiatic Science takes the whole man into account, not just one part of his being or one organ: the liver, spleen or heart. Hippocrates said, a long time ago, that a disorder in one part of the body always meant that the whole organism was perturbed. So the first thing to do is to restore harmony to the whole, and then the part that is ill will be cured by the organism itself. In any case, one thing is certain, and that is that whatever remedies man may try, however many pills, injections and antibiotics he takes, they will always be ineffectual as long as he continues to cultivate inner disorder by his thoughts and feelings.

I cannot agree, either, with methods that separate beings and objects from the whole, from the universe, in order to study and analyse them, for they only succeed in killing the objects of their study. This is no way to reach accurate conclusions! Analysis and dissection are very poor methods. As I have often said, one must never cut things off from the tree of life in order to study them. If you separate something from its source of beauty, light, radiance and vitality, you inevitably destroy it and reduce it to the state of a cadaver. And this is what science studies: cadavers. It has not yet learned to study life. True, I sometimes analyse things myself, but when I do so it is as a preliminary step leading up to a synthesis; I never stop at analysis, for analysis destroys.

If you take a watch apart you will know exactly how it was put together, but it will cease to function. Scientists know exactly what elements man is composed of, but they are incapable of putting all those elements together and producing a human being, a living, thinking being capable of walking and doing things. All the elements may be there, but the essential factor, life, is absent. And only life knows the exact quantities and combinations, and all the conditions necessary for a human organism to function smoothly. So we have to call on life; only life knows how to restore balance to each organ: stomach, brain and lungs, and to the whole body. But as scientists are not concerned with life and are only interested in matter, they will never be able to do this. As long as they cannot rid themselves of their materialistic and mechanistic philosophy which makes them separate the parts from the cosmic whole, they will never succeed in freeing mankind from disease. To be sure, many scientists have a noble ideal, they make a great many sacrifices, they have extraordinary gifts of intelligence and skill, but their philosophy is false, and this is why so many things still escape them.

All that I reveal to you is in harmony with this sublime philosophy that has been entrusted to me and which will, one day, become the philosophy of the whole world. Already, science is finding itself obliged to turn, more and more, to the truths of the past. Let me give you just one example: chemists have long scoffed at alchemists who claimed to be able to transmute lead into gold, but not so long ago, they discovered that an atom of lead had eighty-two electrons and an atom of gold seventy-nine, which means that if they could simply remove three electrons, three protons and a few neutrons from an atom of lead it would become an atom of gold! Of course, it is not feasible to make any quantity of gold in this way; in the first place it would be unstable and, in the second place, the process would be much too costly. But orthodox science has been a little shaken in its beliefs recently, and it is beginning to take an interest in such things as phrenology, telepathy and divining. Before long, it will also begin to acknowledge the existence of astrology. One day everybody will be able to see, hear and read about all these truths that I have been revealing to you for years. More and more, scientists will come to realize that the Ancients, who had neither telescopes nor microscopes, made many extremely important discoveries (who taught them?), and when they come to study the teachings of the Initiates seriously, all their theories will be revolutionized. When this happens, the present situation will be completely reversed: instead of analysis and death, they will teach synthesis and the science of life, and then the Kingdom of God will become possible. But as long as the prevailing materialistic science has not been replaced by the Science of Initiates, the present disorder will prevail.

And yet, now that I have heard the President of France speaking on television about universal brotherhood, for the first time in history, I know that the idea is bound to spread. You heard him, too, didn't you? Ah, yes! When he spoke like that he appeared very great and luminous. It will stick in people's minds. Of course, I know that this idea still speaks, as it were, in a stifled whisper; it is too soon to expect any very striking results. But the whole world has heard it now, and it will continue to make progress. It has a brilliant future ahead of it! One day, when a lot of other people start to express it, it will seem so normal and obvious that everyone will be convinced.

Now I want to show you why the kind of medicine recommended by Initiatic Science is so much better than all the others. As almost all doctors study in medical schools which give priority to the physical dimension, they neglect the other dimension, the way their patients live, and their thoughts, feelings and general behaviour, and yet it is these factors that should have priority. The only true therapy is the way one lives! All the other factors take second, third or fourth place! A human being is composed of a body and of what is known as a 'psyche', and psychosomatic medicine studies the connection between the psychic and the physical in man, and how they relate to and influence each other. Psychosomatic medicine is gaining ground, and this is all to the good! But it will be far more effective when it is founded on a philosophy, on the true overall view of reality of which I propose to sketch the main outlines for you now.

Before anything else, it is essential to have an accurate idea of what a human being is. Man is the foundation on which everything else rests. No true progress can be achieved in any area whatever (scientific, economic, social, psychological or medical), as long as the structure of man, the forces that inhabit him and his relations with the universe are ignored or unknown.

This is the Esoteric Science that Initiates studied, already, thousands of years ago. A great many scientists envisage man as a kind of machine. For a long time, in fact, their approach was purely 'mechanistic'; they would have rejected any suggestion that a human being was inhabited by forces, entities and intelligences still unknown to them, and that these living forces in man were capable of producing new elements which had not hitherto existed in his organism. They still do not know that man possesses several subtle bodies: the etheric, astral, Causal, Buddhic and Atmic bodies. They have no idea of the true nature of thought or of the will... and even less of the soul and the spirit and their inherent powers.[2] In view of all these shortcomings, how can they imagine, for an instant, that they are going to cure human beings? It is quite impossible! Yes, of course, the physical dimension is extremely important, but one also has to look at the higher dimensions, at the higher planes on which other forces and entities exist. What I am saying to you is based on genuine knowledge and, one day, mankind will be obliged to recognize this. A human being is much more than the visible, tangible being before us, but he does not know himself... and medical science does not know him either! Yes, medical science is still treating beings that it does not understand: how can it hope for good results?

So, the first thing to do is to study man, for man is the key to the universe. As long as you do not possess that key, you will find yourself faced with insoluble problems. It is time that scientists and scholars gave man himself the highest priority; when they do so they will discover his invisible dimensions: his aura, his emanations and vibrations, his symbiotic relationship with the entities of nature and the different worlds, his power to travel through space, to tune in to waves, to see and act at a distance, etc. And then everything will be changed. When you are concerned with man, you are at the very heart of things, for man is truly the key to all mysteries.

[2] See *Man's Subtle Bodies and Centres*, Izvor Collection, N° 219, chap. 3.

And now, which therapeutic techniques should be given first place? Those that I have mentioned so far: chemotherapy, phytotherapy, thalassotherapy, chiropractic, are not the most important. The best and most efficacious therapy is to think, feel and act in harmony with the luminous forces and beings of nature and the whole universe.

This means that men must understand these forces and entities, and attune himself to them. This is the sovereign form of medicine. I do not reject the other forms; they are also necessary. But they must always come second to the way one lives, that is to say, to the way one thinks, feels, believes, loves and nourishes oneself. Yes, even to the way one nourishes oneself, for nourishment is not simply a question of eating: we have to know how to eat in such a way that it becomes a process beneficial to us on every plane.

Unfortunately, when you listen to doctors being interviewed on television or on the radio, you never hear them mention the way people live: they only talk about their new treatments, vaccines, radiation therapy, operations, etc. Those who listen to them get the impression that they can continue to live as they please and commit every sort of excess, without regard for laws or rules of any kind. What does it matter? The doctors will find ways of curing them and allowing them to go on living their untidy lives! Yes, and this is why governments will be obliged to go on spending billions and billions on new laboratories and hospitals, until men discover, at last, that what matters most is the way they live.

To be sure, one cannot help but admire some of these doctors: their discoveries and the sacrifices they make are extraordinary! And yet, one is obliged to admit that much of their effort is wasted because they do not know in what direction to look.

Some of you may feel like objecting that, if good or bad health depended on the way we lived, children should never be ill, because they have not had time to have evil thoughts and

Medical Science Must be Based on Initiatic Science

feelings or to do anything wrong. At first sight, this seems to be quite true, but only if you do not know that we all live on this earth more than once. When a child is ill it is because of the way he lived in previous incarnations: if he has been born into a family from whom he inherits certain defects or weaknesses, it is because this is what he has deserved.

As long as you have never studied Initiatic Science, you are bound to draw erroneous conclusions. But this rule is always valid: the most important factor is the way we live, the way we think and feel and act. As long as you have still not understood this, not only will you be unable to straighten out your present lives, but you will be preparing very unfavourable conditions for your future incarnations. It is in your interest to accept these truths taught by the great Initiates. Tell yourselves, 'There are so many things that I still don't understand, but at least I can make up my mind to trust this divine Science, and give priority to the way I live.' After that, you can add all the other forms of therapy you like: but the way you live comes first!

There is yet another form of therapy which I referred to in passing, a few moments ago, and that is the therapy of the sun. One day, the whole of mankind will turn for healing to the sun, which is an inexhaustible reservoir; it is the sun that will effect the most complete cures but, here again, only if we begin by living as we should: the way we live will always be the foremost therapy. When mankind lives according to the laws of God, he will not need clinics and hospitals any longer. At the moment, the only solution seems to be to build more and more hospitals, because there are more and more sick people and more and more varieties of disease. Yes, because the way men live and think is becoming worse and worse. They are becoming more and more knowledgeable and learned, but their health is getting worse and worse. It is very worrying, for on the one hand there is progress, while on the other there is... what can I call it: degeneration? And it is no good thinking that the situation can be remedied by material elements, for God has not given the gift of absolute efficacy to matter: matter can never provide more than a temporary relief.

Human beings give their physical bodies the food and drink they need, but man is more than a physical body: he is also a soul and a spirit, and the soul and spirit cannot be fed on meat and potatoes... or hormones! And as science makes no provision for the needs of men's souls and spirits, they are left to suffer from hunger and thirst. This is why we see so many people who, apparently, have everything they could possibly need: a good job, a family, a house and car, etc., and yet, deep down, they feel an emptiness, they are dissatisfied. This is a sure sign that they have forgotten their soul; as for their spirit, it just doesn't come into it! The medicine of the future will be obliged to take into account all the needs of human beings, including those of the soul and spirit, and to supply them with the elements lacking to them.

So, my dear brothers and sisters, our Teaching will give you neither houses nor cars nor fine clothes, but you will find in it all that you need to satisfy your soul and spirit. And when the soul and spirit are satisfied, they have a beneficial effect on the physical body and new processes are set in motion. And then, even if your physical body is not very well dressed or has not had much to eat, it can hold up its head with self-respect. Yes, our Teaching gives you the most precious and indispensable elements you need for equilibrium and happiness.

It is well known that many patients would be cured if their doctor would only give them just a few kind words, but as he is always in a hurry, he writes a prescription and rushes off to his next appointment. Many doctors think that love, hope and encouragement are not important; in fact, they often actually kill their patients by telling them that they have only a few days to live. Fortunately, there are some who realize that it is important to have a friendly relationship with their patients; they know that medicines are not the only things that can work a cure. In the past, many doctors were true apostles, but nowadays, unfortunately, as often as not, they are mere mercenaries. In fact, in the United States, there are patients who never even see a doctor: their illness is diagnosed by electronic machines and, depending on the results, the patient may see the doctor or, equally, he may not, in which case he will receive his prescription by post! Yes, there is no more human contact; everything is automated and love goes by the board. And yet, the only thing that heals is love!

One day, all this will change and men will discover that it is love, trust and hope that is so sorely missing, that the cause of all their ill health is doubt, distrust and disharmony. This is why I repeat and insist that the most potent of all therapies is the way you live. To be sure, I cannot promise you that its curative effects will be as rapid as those of a drug. When you take some pills, you feel the effects almost at once. But do they last? And can you continue to take pills without suffering from side effects? The kind of medicine I am prescribing acts slowly, but it is safer and, in the long run, it is the most effective. The only condition is that it presupposes a truthful, authentic, all-embracing philosophy of life.

And when I speak of philosophy, I am referring to the one and only philosophy which was not elaborated by the human intellect, but was discovered by the great Initiates, thanks to their gifts of clairvoyance and astral projection. And I can tell you this: Heaven has chosen me to be one of the heirs to this divine philosophy. Without it, it is impossible to find the true path; we shall always lose our way. This is why I give absolute priority to this philosophy, for it teaches man how to live in harmony with all the different forces and worlds that exist, so that he need no longer be torn apart by inner conflict and contradiction. It reveals, also, how man is constructed and what exchanges his soul and spirit need to make with the forces of nature. For the physical body, breathing is an indispensable form of exchange; if man is deprived of this he dies. And he dies, too, if his soul and spirit are not allowed to breathe, that is, if his soul and spirit are never given the opportunity to give and receive from the cosmos.

Now, therefore, go back and refresh your memory of all the rules and formulas that I have already given you, and remember to put yourselves in touch with the forces of nature: when you do this you will be given the light to see the universe as an edifice, the most marvellous edifice imaginable, in which everything, from the summit to the base, is connected; when you see this more clearly, you will be capable of restoring order and remedying many of the anomalies within you. Why can't you appreciate the value of all the truths I have given you? Because I am not famous or well known? As far as I am concerned, fame is not important: the only thing that matters is to discover truth. I have given my whole life to this and I cannot say that I am particularly interested in all the rest: fame and recognition. Besides, recognition will come without my having to look for it, for when you possess the truth, sooner or later, you receive recognition. And if you are in error, that, too, will always be recognized in the end: even if everyone applauds you now, one day you will simply be forgotten. No, no; I am working for something that can never be either replaced or forgotten.

What matters most, therefore, is to learn how to live, think, feel and act. On other occasions I have explained the process by which plants and fishes, and even babies in their mother's womb, were formed. You will remember that I explained the law of affinity, and showed you how man's thoughts and feelings linked him to kindred entities, forces and elements in space, and how, ultimately, these entities and forces came and attached themselves to him. Yes, it is an absolute law that man attracts to himself whatever he has formed ties with, and in this law can be found the explanation for all health or sickness, strength or weakness, intelligence or stupidity, beauty or ugliness, and so on. They are simply elements that we have attracted to ourselves.

This means that, if you are experiencing difficulties in your present life, it is certainly because of your ignorance in the past which caused you to perturb the right order of things. But now, thanks to this Initiatic philosophy which teaches you how to work at improving your thoughts and desires, you are in a position to form ties with the most highly spiritual entities and regions, and build a new body that will manifest all the qualities you want: health, strength and beauty. This is the secret of resurrection. If you are willing to understand and apply this science of life, you will have the power not only to defend yourselves against disease, but also to rebuild your body as you would like it to be. To be sure, for the time being, it may resist your efforts, but that is because, unconsciously, you have been working for hundreds of years to defile it, so it is going to take a long time to restore it to perfect health. But the law that I have stated is absolute. Six or seven years are sufficient to get a degree in medicine, but the Science of life is so vast that it takes thousands of years to possess it!

When men finally understand the needs of the soul and spirit, they will see that they have to be awakened and given some work to do. Everything else depends on this work, for all causes are in the soul and spirit: all the rest is a consequence. When you know that you are working on the level of causes (the level at which forces are set in motion), you can live in peace and certainty, for you also know the effects which are bound to follow. And this is how we can begin to cure psychic illness: by giving men knowledge and certainty. It is because man is not conscious of the fact that his soul and spirit are in touch with the luminous forces of nature that he is disorientated and tormented and has this sense of emptiness. Once light dawns in him, it reveals his links with Immensity and Eternity, and he realizes that he is capable of communicating with the forces of the cosmos and of transforming his life. And then, certainty and joy are his constant companions. If you do not enlighten people it is almost useless to try to heal them. They need this light, and they need it from earliest childhood. You can only help human beings to solve their physical and psychic problems by teaching them the truth about their own nature, and by showing them how they are linked to the Tree of Life and how they can draw strength from it to work and transform themselves.

Never forget this: you must give absolute priority to this philosophy and to the way you live, and, on the physical plane, it is the sun that must take priority. One day, science will study the question of how the sun can cure one: at what time of day and for how long one should sunbathe; how to expose water to the light of the sun, in bottles of different colours, and at what time of day to drink it; how to work with sunlight in all its forms, and how to use certain instruments to extract the curative elements contained in the sun. How wonderful when that day comes! At the moment, science attaches little importance to the sun because it is only interested in matter, in the chemical elements. And yet, if sea water, seaweed, herbs and trees, and even gems and crystals, can cure, it is because they have received their curative powers from the sun. The sun will be the last to be appreciated, but once man discovers it, he will be obliged to give it priority: men will eat and drink the sun, breathe the sun, and even listen to the music of the sun, for they will have equipment capable of tuning in to it. Yes, the most beautiful music is that which comes from the sun. The most excellent messages, also, and, one day, men will be able to listen to the sun's broadcasts. Are you wondering whether I am talking seriously? Yes, I am not joking: I am speaking absolutely seriously.

When I was in the Pyrenees in October and November, the air was so pure and the sun shone as though it were springtime, and I was able to see it rise every morning. Then I realized that I needed to eat less: I was nourished by the air and the sun. I ate once a day, anyway, because I did not want to undernourish my body, but I did not really feel the need to eat. So then I thought that I would repeat an experience which I had already had in the past, when I fasted for two weeks. It is amazing how many things I discovered! During my fast I read, meditated and wrote, but I also worked for hours out of doors, digging and pruning and tidying up this little bit of land. I continued to watch the sun rising until December. But before the sun rose, the sky was tinted with the most extraordinary and beautiful colours: gold, orange and pink. I filmed some of them. One morning in particular, the whole sky, from east to west, was completely pink; I had never seen anything like it. The pure air, the cloudless sky, the view of the mountains, the peace and stillness and the thoughts of love that I sent out in all directions, all nourished me. This just shows that man's real need is for things of a subtle nature.

Yes, in my view, the therapy of the future will be the therapy of the sun, and we shall apply it by watching the sunrise, by forming a bond of affection with the sun, by concentrating strongly on it in order to receive its particles. Science still knows nothing about the etheric particles that abound in every ray of sunlight. And yet, although modern medical science has still not acknowledged the existence of the more subtle aspects of matter, it has already realized that the most important elements in the body, and for the health of the body, are those that are imponderable. After attempting to cure the ailments of the digestive, circulatory, respiratory and excretory systems of their patients... in other words, after attempting to treat the organs, they finally discovered the endocrine glands whose imperceptible secretions block or stimulate the activity of the organs.

But the endocrine glands are not the be-all and end-all of scientific discovery: they, in turn, depend on other, subtler centres and, ultimately, on thought. It is as though the thought processes themselves contained glands which controlled the whole physical organism. One day, science will discover that there is a hierarchical structure that embraces every level of human existence, from thought to the physical organs. Yes, I don't believe that the endocrine glands are the most important, for they themselves depend on other factors. Man injures or improves his physical health by means of his thoughts and feelings which act on his glandular system. Growth or the cessation of growth, increase or loss of weight, etc., cannot be attributed only to the action of the endocrine glands.

It is interesting to note that science is working with progressively subtler elements. Still in the field of medicine, we find that homoeopathy uses remedies potentized to the 31st centesimal. Anyone would think that there could be no curative power left in them, and yet they are highly effective. And physicists, too, are discovering aspects of matter that are more and more subtle: after protons and neutrons, they have now found what they call mesons and neutrinos. When they finally reach the etheric dimension of matter, they will find particles and energies which are still unknown, today, and which originate in the sun. A whole new science will develop for the study of the sun's rays. In fact, instead of buying our vitamins at the chemist's we shall go and get them from the sun. The vitamins that we buy at the pharmacy cannot be properly assimilated by our bodies; it is far better to get them from fruit and vegetables, for that is where the sun has put them. The properties of even the most commonplace vegetables such as onions, leeks and radishes are still largely unknown. Turnips, for instance, are very good for you; and you should also eat the leaves of radishes: they are very tasty and contain more nutrients than the radishes themselves.

To conclude, I want to tell you, again, that if you know how to breathe, eat and drink, you will get your vitamins from the world around you, from all those elements in which the sun has concealed them. For the most important factor of all is the psychological attitude with which you receive things. You can swallow vitamin pills from morning until night, but if you have the wrong attitude, they will not make you any stronger. In fact, they will probably cause other problems in your digestive or circulatory system. Doctors never talk about the importance of their patients' state of consciousness or of the positive attitude they should have towards things: this is why the medicines they prescribe are even less effective than they might be. So, here again, you have a vitally important factor: our inner attitude towards what we receive.

Many brothers and sisters tell me, 'Master, when I am with you, I think and feel and act differently; problems seem to disappear; everything goes swimmingly! But as soon as I have been away from you for any length of time, nothing is the same: I find myself back in the workaday reality of life; I seem to be less convinced about the Teaching, and I can remember almost nothing of all that you told us.' And my reply is that I experienced exactly the same thing, when I was young, in relation to my own Master, Peter Deunov. But if I am with you, now, it is in order to help you not only to accept a certain number of truths, but also to make an effort to keep them alive within you for as long as possible. Life is terribly hard, you say? Don't I know it! We constantly have to struggle, to face up to difficulties of all kinds, and we get tired! Yes, I know: life is difficult. I shall not explain why it is like that at the moment, but if I am with you it is in order to make you understand that if you accept the light of this Teaching, you will be much stronger and more courageous, and you will always know peace and hope.

When you go home, therefore, make an effort to keep the truths that you have received here vibrant and alive within you. Don't forget them. Tell yourself: 'I know that I can't escape from the realities of everyday life, but I must cling to these truths so as to be on the look-out when hesitation, discouragement and negative thoughts come along. Whatever happens I will not give in; I refuse to be dragged down; I refuse to throw away my enthusiasm and hope! I will not let my flame be snuffed out.' Yes, cling to the truths I give you, take a few deep breaths of oxygen and then take the plunge and go and face reality! In this way you will be strong and very powerful, and become a source of life. Isn't that much better?

So many of you say, 'Yes, I understand! From now on I'll be stronger. You'll see!' And then, when difficulties arise, they give up the struggle once again. When they come back here, of course, they are ashamed of their weakness, and resolve to do better in future: 'You'll just see; I'll not give in.' No, not until next time! So, the wisest solution is to keep coming back until you really do become staunch and unshakeable. This is what the Teaching is all about: becoming unshakeable and, whatever the circumstances, remembering that you are immortal and that God has given you every possibility you need. If you forget this, it will be the end of you!

My dear brothers and sisters, try to understand what I am saying! I can hear you thinking, 'But we do, we do!' No, I'm afraid you don't; not yet! You have not yet reached the kind of understanding that I am talking about. To understand me means to be as firm as a rock in your convictions. Some of you have this firmness, but not all. As soon as they find themselves back in the turmoil of life or, as in this Christmas season, for instance, when they see the shops overflowing with good things, their philosophy goes flying out of the window, and they can think only of what they want to buy or to receive for Christmas. Immediately, it is as though they had no more faith, no religion, no God. Don't you think that I have seen the shops, too? But when I see them I say to myself, 'Oh, that's magnificent. Wonderful! But it's for others, not for me. I have something else!'

The only thing that interests me is this philosophy that I patiently continue to transmit to you, and which can give you infinite possibilities of evolution. Any philosophy, in fact, that fails to recognize that man has an infinite capacity for growth is incapable of teaching him the true meaning of life. You must not follow such philosophies.

Christmas is almost here, my dear brothers and sisters. I have not said very much about light, today, but take what I have said and think about it. A great many things will disappear without a trace, but the elements of Initiatic Science that I reveal to you will endure for ever.

Sèvres, 23 December 1967

Chapter Three

THE FUTURE OF MEDICINE

Question: *Master, what future do you see for medicine, from the point of view of your Teaching?*

The future of medicine? Why, it is going to be brilliant! Wonderful! Doctors will all be out of work. That makes you laugh, but it is true: they will have nothing to do because there will be no more sick people. And in the meantime? Yes, of course, in the meantime they will not lack for work for, in view of the way people live, not only will there be more and more sick people, but there will also be more and more new diseases.

When you see all the progress that has been made in surgical techniques, radiation treatment and so on, one cannot deny that modern medicine in the West is very impressive. But why is it that, far from getting better, more and more people are falling ill? Sometimes, I wonder if there are two really healthy people in the whole world! And the list of known diseases is getting longer and longer. Oh, I know: you will tell me that these diseases have always existed, but that we just did not know about them. Well, there is some truth in that, but it is not entirely true. And nor can I agree with so many who say that the new illnesses are due to polluted air and water and adulterated foods:

that, too, is only partially true. To be sure, factories release industrial wastes into the waterways, the air is fouled by smoke and toxic gasses, fruit and vegetables are cultivated with massive doses of chemical fertilizers, and the bread, butter, oil and everything else we eat, has been processed and tampered with! But all that is only the material aspect of the question, and the true causes of disease lie elsewhere: in the way human beings think and feel and behave. But you will never hear anyone talking about this; no one ever explains that certain thoughts and feelings putrefy and can poison you. So everyone attempts to remedy their ailments by swallowing medicines, without realizing that it is their thoughts and feelings that destroy or restore their health.

Psychosomatic medicine saw the light of day only recently; twenty or thirty years ago; and this is a sign that doctors are, at last, beginning to recognize the role of the human psyche in illness and to explore the subtler aspects of man. But this subtle aspect is nothing new: it has always existed! So why do so many doctors still obstinately refuse to envisage anything but the material, physical aspects of illness? Forty or fifty years ago, it was thought that the only thing that mattered was the number of calories the body needed to function properly; the discussion centred on the proteins, lipids, carbohydrates and mineral salts contained in our daily diet. After this, came the discovery of vitamins, and the spotlight was switched from calories to vitamins, which have the advantage of being needed only in minute doses and of being far more potent than proteins and carbohydrates. And now, the latest discovery is the endocrine glands and the extremely subtle hormones they secrete, which are even more important than vitamins!

But for all their importance, the endocrine glands are not ultimately responsible for everything that goes on in our bodies: they only carry out orders received from elsewhere, and if, as sometimes happens, they secrete too much or too little, or cease to function altogether, it is because they are conditioned by other, much subtler factors, which medical research has not yet discovered. Oh, yes, there are still many things to be discovered! It is the invisible dimension that is in command of the visible, the subtle world that is in command of the physical, the spirit that is in command of matter. But our contemporaries still refuse to accept this. They believe that the subtle, psychic dimension is commanded by the material dimension, the physical body, and that thoughts, for example, are secreted by the brain just as bile is secreted by the liver. In fact it is the exact opposite, for thoughts are living beings[1]. But I cannot go into that now; I have already talked to you about it, and I want to stick to your question

After a period in which it gave exaggerated importance to chemical remedies, medicine is beginning to swing back towards more natural remedies, for it has gradually seen how drugs paralyse the body's healthy reactions. The body must be given the possibility of defending itself; it already possesses the means to do so, but the frequent use of chemical substances inhibits its functions and prevents it from manufacturing the antibodies it needs to cure itself. Look at how an animal reacts to illness: it does not take antibiotics, it goes off all by itself and rests, or it finds the herb it needs to cure itself. But when a man is ill, doctors stuff him with drugs until his system is paralysed and incapable of reacting. As a matter of fact, it is already recognized by almost all doctors, that antibiotics and radiation – ultraviolet, infra-red, cobalt rays, and so on – all have very harmful side effects.

Doctors experiment with new treatments without fully foreseeing the reactions that are liable to follow; in fact, many patients serve as guinea-pigs without knowing it. Or they use real guinea-pigs or other animals; but what is good for animals is not necessarily good for human beings. What makes you think that a treatment that is successful on a mouse or a rabbit

---

1 See *Izvor Collection*, N° 224, chap. 4.

will necessarily be successful when applied to a human being? The structure of human beings is quite different from that of mice or rabbits! Besides, men do not have the right to kill thousands and thousands of animals for experimentation. It is a crime that humanity will have to pay for one day. If you read Genesis, you will see that it was only in the time of Noah that God allowed men to kill animals. The only food that Adam and Eve were allowed to eat was fruit and herbs. Later on, after they left the Ark, when men had already lost their first innocence and light, the Lord allowed them to slaughter animals for food, while forbidding them to shed human blood, saying: 'Surely for your lifeblood I will demand a reckoning'! Well, for my part, I think that the blood of animals must also be paid for, and that many new illnesses are the result of this indiscriminate slaughter of animals. One day, men will be required to shed as much of their own blood as they have shed of the blood of animals. It is only justice. But let us leave this question for the moment...

What will medicine be like in the future? Well, in the first place, people will understand more and more clearly that each human being already possesses the elements he needs to resist disease. Yes, there are cases of people who were considered terminally ill by their doctors and who have managed to cure themselves. How? By will-power and thought. Of course, it is not everyone who can do this, you have to have developed certain faculties; but it is possible. I have already spoken to you, in another lecture, of plants whose roots are not planted in the soil: they draw their vitality from the atmosphere. How can they do this? Well, if a plant is capable of getting all the elements it needs from the atmosphere in this way, how much more should man be capable of doing the same! Chemists will say, 'It's a question of chemical processes, it's purely chemical...' Yes, to be sure, everything is chemical, but chemistry is commanded by the spirit. The spirit is capable of producing curative chemical elements, but medical science still refuses to recognize these powers of the spirit, and this is where its great error lies.

Instead of pursuing more and more daring experiments in chemical and surgical techniques, research should take other directions: the physical environment of the sick, for instance, should be very different. They should be surrounded by colours and sounds that would help to awaken their dormant powers. Human beings have the innate capacity to neutralize anything that could harm them, but they have not got the knowledge or will-power they need to put this capacity to work; in other words, it is the spiritual dimension that is deficient. Nothing is missing on the material, physical level: there have never been so many hospitals, clinics and pharmacies! None of that existed in the past. It is amazing to see the resources that exist nowadays, and yet, in spite of it all, there are more and more sick people.

The medicine of the future will teach human beings to find the curative elements they need on the etheric plane. Yes, all the chemical elements that we now buy at the chemist's shop in the form of medicines, exist in the etheric state, in the atmosphere. This is where men will learn to find them, and they will breathe them in and take as much as they need without danger. In the future, human beings will take less and less of all those drugs that end by poisoning them: they will get the curative elements they need from the sun, the air, the sea, trees and mountains, as well as from colours, music, words and movements, thoughts and feelings. The potential efficacy of all these things has still not really been studied.

The extent to which the conceptions of human beings have been influenced by materialism is very evident in certain areas, particularly in the area of the education and training of the young. People believe that in order to instruct the young and fit them for their future responsibilities in life, they have to improve school buildings and equipment, build swimming pools and stadiums, etc. And where does that get them? Obviously, as far as the sheer sum of knowledge or memory training are concerned, it is true: young people are very advanced... although, I must say that one hears more and more teachers complaining that their pupils know nothing! But their character and their mentality in general are deplorable! In the past, there was never enough of anything in schools. Sometimes there were no books or pencils; there was no glass in the windows, and each child had to bring a log to school, otherwise there would have been no heat! And yet these schools turned out geniuses, leaders and men who were models of nobility. Why? Because the whole of their education focused on behaviour and character, in other words: on the spiritual dimension.

Yes, as I have said: the future of medicine is unemployment! As far as I am concerned, anyway, I know a way of ensuring that every doctor will be out of a job. How? It is very simple. I shall pick out a large and very beautiful property in the country, and there I shall have some houses built according to the indications I shall give as to form and colour. There will be masses of flowers, paintings and statues and so on, and pregnant women will be housed and fed free of charge for the duration of their pregnancy. Everything will be made as easy as possible for them. They will listen to lectures and concerts and spend a lot of time on a spiritual work which will influence the children they are carrying. Naturally, their husbands will come to see them, and they, too, will listen to some talks. There! That is how to bring children into the world who will never know a day's illness! Today, they are ill because their poor mothers have to put up with so much during the nine months of gestation. Many families have to huddle together with others in a dark, confined slum with a filthy yard in which everybody hangs out their washing. The husband comes home, drunk or discouraged because he has no job, and starts beating his pregnant wife... How can you expect the children to turn out well in these conditions?

Naturally, the situation is not always so tragic; I know that. But it is still true that if parents have children who fall ill or turn to crime, it is because they do not know how to bring them into the world. If young girls and boys would only read what I said thirty years ago, already, about the mysteries of galvanoplasty, they would understand how this process is repeated in every area, particularly in the case of gestation[2]. They would understand the elements that correspond, in a pregnant woman, to the solution of metallic salts, the anode and cathode, etc., and they would know how to produce magnificent children. You must read that lecture. Yes, when I see how many billions the State is wasting on hospitals, prisons and law courts, I tell myself that, if only it would agree, I could save it a fantastic amount of money, because it is possible to organize things in such a way as to ensure that there be no more sick people and no more criminals. And now, are you going to tell me that all that is not scientific? There is nothing more scientific than what I have just been saying!

What will become of all the doctors when they have no more sick people to care for? They will be poets, dancers, painters, musicians: anything you like! Everybody will be fit and healthy, everybody will enjoy life, everybody will dance and sing and travel all over the world to contemplate beauty wherever it is to be found. You will probably say, 'I can't believe all that; you're dreaming!' Yes and no. To be sure, when one sees how people manifest themselves today, when one sees what interests them and what their ambitions are, one cannot help but think that most of them will simply continue to live as they are living now, in the same disorder and with the same illnesses. But when one knows that human beings possess extraordinary faculties which have not yet begun to manifest themselves, one cannot avoid the conviction that everything is possible as long as they are willing to study these faculties and work to develop them.

---

[2] See *Education Begins Before Birth*, Izvor Collection, N° 203, chaps. 1, 2 and 3.

As long as medical science has no real understanding of the human structure, it will never really cure illness, particularly psychic illnesses: psychoses and schizophrenia and so on, for in these cases it is not the physical, but the subtle bodies that are out of order. This is why the very first thing doctors should know is that, beyond his physical body, man possesses other bodies of a subtle nature: the etheric body which permeates the physical body and which is the seat of memory and the emotions; the astral body, that is, the body of feelings and emotions, and the mental body... But I have already spoken to you at length about man's different bodies: etheric, astral, mental, Causal, Buddhic and Atmic, and I am not going to dwell on that today. I have also spoken to you about the Body of Glory, also known as the Body of Light or of Immortality, the Body of Christ[3]. The most important work of Initiatic Science is to form this body, for it is this that enables man to enter eternity.

Human beings attach far too much importance to the physical body, their own and that of others. I have often told you the story of the multi-millionaire who gave his wife all the most expensive presents: villas, cars, furs and jewellery, only to find, one day, that she had gone off with his chauffeur! Why? Because all those gifts were for the satisfaction of her physical body. He had never given her anything to satisfy her heart or soul, never anything spiritual, never any of those things that cannot be seen but that are so keenly felt. Yes, of course, his wife had a soul, but he never thought about that. He only thought about satisfying her physical body, so her poor soul was wilting and dying of hunger while her body was sated. What poverty to think that the physical body is the most important! This is my major criticism of materialistic ideologies: they are

---

[3] See *Christmas and Easter in the Initiatic Tradition*, Izvor Collection, N° 209, chap 6.

only interested in material well-being, work, food and housing. They never take into consideration the needs of the soul and spirit.

So I warn you, my dear brothers and sisters: discard this materialistic philosophy, for it can only weaken you and drag you down to the level of animals. You can see this with your own eyes in someone who is convinced that he is made only of matter, that the soul does not exist, that there is no life after death: he is capable of every ignoble act, and no wonder! How can you expect anything else? But the real tragedy is that when you put all these ideas into his head you destroy his will to do something sublime, you destroy the power of the spirit. In other words, you kill him! Whereas if you could get him to realize that he possesses a spirit and that, by giving his spirit the opportunity to manifest itself, he would be capable of greatness, you would be putting real power into his hands: his body would begin to obey him and respect his orders; he would no longer be bowled over by privations, misfortunes or illness; he would grow every day in strength and power and become a leader for the whole world to follow! But if he adopts the philosophy of materialism, he will be nothing. This is the danger of giving priority to the physical body, to matter, to the external, objective dimension. To be sure, you will not see the full extent of the damage at once, but little by little, the human being sickens and dies. Reread the lecture about the strength of the spirit[4]; you will find all the elements you need in order to advance and overcome all your difficulties. Yes, the philosophy you must adopt, henceforth, is that of the spirit. Don't listen to stupid, ignorant people who try to drag you down into the dust. It is true, we are matter, we are made of dust, but only part of us: the other part is divine.

I have already said this, but let me repeat it: as long as medical science does not know man and his different bodies, it

---

[4] See *Complete Works*, vol. 5, chap. 8.

will never be capable of saving him. Take the case of someone whose etheric body is not properly attached to his physical body: he will feel that something is wrong, but the doctors will be unable to find the cause of his discomfort, for his physical body is perfectly normal. So far, doctors are incapable of treating the etheric body, and as long as they refuse to recognize the existence of man's subtle bodies, it is no use their hoping to achieve the complete cure of disease.

Contemporary medicine, to be sure, has a fantastic range of techniques to choose from: I take my hat off to all that! But I am obliged to repeat that it is very seriously mistaken in many ways, simply because it does not yet know the true nature of man.

Toulouse, 20 December 1970

Chapter Four

A DISCIPLE MUST DEVELOP
HIS SPIRITUAL SENSES

I want to say a few words to you today, particularly for the benefit of those who are here for the first time. I have no doubt, however, that they will also be useful to all the others, for they will give them some arguments to use when talking to people who have not yet understood the importance of the spiritual life.

We all have a physical body, and this physical body is composed of different organs; even babies know that: ask them to show you their eyes and they will point to them; and they can also show you their mouth, their ears, their nose and their podgy little legs! It is amazing how much tiny children know! Later, when they go to school, they learn that man has five senses: sight, smell, hearing, taste and touch. Each of the five senses gives us specific sensations: the sensation provided by the sense of touch is not the same as that procured by taste or sight; this, too, is something that everybody knows. All of man's contacts with the world about him are based on the five senses, and this is why he has a tendency to exploit their possibilities to the full and, particularly, to enhance and amplify the pleasurable sensations provided by his eyes, ears, skin, etc. Amongst the sensations man experiences, some are more necessary than others and some are more intense than others.

Take the sense of taste, for example: who would deny the wealth of variety and the importance of the sensations provided by the sense of taste... especially when you are enjoying a delicious meal! Or take the sense of touch: when a man and woman make love, they experience very intense sensations. So much so, in fact, that it is thought that the most intense sensations are those provided by sexual pleasure. But this is not at all certain. It may be true, in general, but not for everybody: certain artists endowed with very great sensitivity of sight or hearing are far more deeply moved by colours and sounds than by the sexual act which often leaves them indifferent and unmoved. But as the majority of human beings are not so highly evolved, we can truthfully say that the two senses which govern the world today are those of touch (which includes sexuality) and taste. The senses of sight, hearing and smell seem to be relatively unimportant: some people are totally indifferent to scents, sounds and colours unless their personal interests are involved in some way. In this respect they resemble animals that have developed their senses of smell, sight and hearing to such a pitch because it was in their interests to do so: they needed them for their protection and in order to find food.

I am talking about things that you know already, of course, I realize that; but I do so in order to draw your attention to certain conclusions that have certainly never occurred to you. For thousands of years, men have been doing everything in their power to increase the variety and intensity of the sensations and perceptions that enter their consciousness through the channels of their five senses, and it is this play on the keyboard of man's five senses that they call culture and civilization. Well, for my part, I find this rather meagre! However great the degree of refinement of the five senses, they will always be limited because they belong to the physical dimension; they can never explore what lies beyond it. Yes, but nature has plans for adding more keys to this keyboard: a sixth, seventh and even an eighth sense, far more powerful and intense than those we have at present. At the moment, though, men confine themselves to their five physical senses; they are unwilling to admit that there are other dimensions to be explored, other sights, scents and textures to be experienced. So it is not surprising if they are incapable of enjoying new and more varied, richer or more subtle sensations. How can you explain the fact that in the absence of any external stimulus to their physical senses, some people have perceptions that plunge them into ecstasies in which they experience an altered state of consciousness, a sense of fulfilment, majesty and immensity? I know these sensations, I have experienced and tasted them, and they are beyond the power of words to describe!

We have to get human beings to understand that if they keep trying to multiply and amplify only their physical sensations, they are condemning themselves to bitter disappointment, for the scope of these sensations is very limited. Everybody knows that each organ has a particular function: you don't see with your ears, but with your eyes; you don't hear with your eyes, nor with your tongue or your legs, but with your ears. Each organ is specialized: it fills its own specific function and provides us only with the sensations that correspond to its own specific nature. If we want to experience fresh sensations we shall have to turn to other organs which we all possess.

Observe the reactions of human beings: they can look at whatever they please, they can taste or touch or buy whatever they want, and yet they are always dissatisfied. In the course of all my travels, I have met dozens of very rich people who were unhappy, jaded and world-weary! They had tried everything they could think of to alleviate their boredom and misery, but to no avail because they had confined themselves to such limited horizons. I have often used the example of an extremely wealthy man, a magnate of the oil or steel industry, for instance: he gives his wife all the jewels, precious stones and palatial houses imaginable, but she is never satisfied. Why not? Because there is still something within her, something that we call the soul or the spirit, that is being buried and stifled under all that wealth. No one ever thinks that the soul needs to be nourished, too. Everything is for the physical body: 'Here, eat; it's for you!' Our feeling of dissatisfaction does not come from the physical body, and yet it is always the physical body that we inundate with food and presents of every kind. It does not need all that; in fact it needs very little, really. It is our soul and spirit that are perpetually anaemic and dying of hunger! But as people don't realize this (in fact, they don't even know that they have a soul and a spirit!), they continue to cherish and provide only for their physical body, and their problems are never solved: they continue to feel dissatisfied. It is the soul and spirit that need to be provided for.

But what does your soul want? The soul asks for space! For room to breathe and expand. And what about the spirit: what does your spirit ask for? Years ago I gave you a synoptic table which detailed the principal elements of our psychic life: heart, mind, soul and spirit, and the needs and activities of each element.[1] This table is the quintessence of spiritual philosophy. If you want to experience fulfilment and new and tremendously potent and varied sensations, you must no longer rely exclusively on your five senses. In this respect Orientals are capable of experiences that would be unthinkable for a Westerner. In India and Tibet, for example, there are yogis who live in holes in the ground. When I was in the Himalayas I met a disciple of Babaji, called Hanuman Baba. He never said a word, because Babaji had forbidden him to talk for several years, but he used a slate to communicate with others. I spent hours with him; we were often together until two or three in the morning. And he, too, slept in a hole, with just enough room to stretch out in. In darkness and complete silence there is no nourishment for the five senses and, by constant meditation, the yogi succeeds in rendering them numb and inactive. And once

---

[1] See *Complete Works*, vol. 13, chap. 10.

The Synoptic Table

PRINCIPLE	IDEAL	NOURISHMENT	PRICE	ACTIVITY
SPIRIT DIVINE CONSCIOUSNESS	TIME ETERNITY IMMORTALITY	FREEDOM	TRUTH	UNION CREATION IDENTIFICATION
SOUL SUPER-CONSCIOUSNESS	SPACE IMMENSITY INFINITY	IMPERSONALITY SELFLESSNESS	FUSION DILATATION ECSTASY	CONTEMPLATION ADORATION PRAYER
INTELLECT SELF-CONSCIOUSNESS	KNOWLEDGE LEARNING LIGHT	THOUGHT	WISDOM	MEDITATION PROFOUND STUDY
HEART CONSCIOUSNESS	JOY HAPPINESS WARMTH	FEELINGS	LOVE	MUSIC SONG POETRY HARMONY
WILL SUBCONSCIOUS	DOMINATION POWER MOVEMENT	STRENGTH	GESTURES BREATH	BREATHING GYMNASTICS DANCE PANEURYTHMY
PHYSICAL BODY UNCONSCIOUS	VIGOUR HEALTH LIFE	FOOD	MONEY	ACTIVITY DYNAMISM WORK

the senses cease their activity, they no longer absorb the psychic energy intended for the subtle force-centres, so these centres can be awakened and the yogi begins to see, hear, smell and touch the fluidic elements of the higher realms of reality.

Westerners have honed the five senses to a high degree of perfection, and they are convinced that it is in this way that they will know all there is to know and attain happiness! They know a great deal, to be sure, and they experience a wide variety of sensations, but their five senses devour every available drop of psychic energy so that they have none left for the spiritual dimension. In the West, people live too much on the level of their physical sensations; they don't have the energy to awaken and develop their other dormant faculties of perception. Too many sensations! You only have to look at young people. Adults are generally more moderate, because they have finally understood that they get no real benefit from living like that, but the young are avid for every kind of sensation. They want to see and hear everything, they want to meet and embrace and quarrel and scream... and they think that that is life! But it is only one aspect of life. They are alive, to be sure, but they are alive with a life which conceals true life. You must understand this before you can make up your minds to exclude from your lives many different sensations which make true understanding and true intuition impossible. It is not good to live in a glut of sensations. People are plunged, as it were, in an ocean that is constantly being whipped to a fury by gales of excitement and agitation. They are incapable of remaining for a few minutes in silence, of raising their thoughts to a higher level and experiencing sensations of a totally different nature and a different quality. They always look for their sensations on too low a level; they should look for them on high.

This is something that I have ascertained for myself, time and time again: it is when one is steeped in silence and meditation, far removed from all physical sensations, that it becomes possible to enter certain subtle regions and slake one's

A Disciple Must Develop His Spiritual Senses

thirst with sensations that can never be experienced on the material plane. Such sensations are an inner experience, and they can only be obtained by the work of thought and will-power. You will say, 'All that is very vague! You talk about extraordinary sensations, but you never explain exactly what these sensations are or how they manifest themselves.' That is true, you are quite right, but it is because they cannot be explained; no one can ever describe them. You have to experience them for yourselves before you can really understand them. I have no words to describe them: I only know that this is the only reality. Yes, the only reality is the life that exists on high and that can only be attained by our souls and spirits.

As you know, we hear a lot about the havoc that drugs are creating, particularly amongst the young: opium, L.S.D., marijuana, cocaine and heroin. Certain drugs have been used traditionally in some Asian or South American countries, but that is quite a different question. What is serious, here, is that young people are using these drugs in order to escape the humdrum reality of their lives and attain higher levels of consciousness, whereas, in fact, all they are doing is destroying themselves. Drugs are exceedingly harmful for the nervous system. Initiates never recommend the use of drugs; in fact they themselves never or rarely use them, and even then only in tiny doses as, for instance, in the case of musk.

Before going to India I knew about the special properties of musk, which you must not confuse with the perfume of the same name, which is a synthetic product. True musk *(muscus officinalis)* is a secretion of the sexual glands of the musk-deer that lives on the high plateaux of Tibet. The odour of this secretion is so strong that it attracts female deer from great distances. When it is dried, it is a little like very small, dark brown, almost black, tea leaves. I know it, because I have used it myself in exceptional circumstances. If they have some particular work to do, some Initiates take a grain or two in hot water with mint, to strengthen their nervous system and solar plexus. Musk is not harmful; it is as though one instilled a drop of fire, of prime matter, into one's body.

When I was in India I learned how to make a paste from the roots of a certain plant combined with red leaves from another kind of plant. These are ground up together on a stone, and the resulting paste is applied in the form of a small red patch on the forehead, between the eyebrows. It is used as an aid to meditation, for it has the property of opening the third eye. If you like, I can give you the names of these plants, but you will not be able to find them easily. Indians and Tibetans know a great deal about plants; it is a science that has been handed down from one generation to the next for thousands of years. The properties of some of the plants in their repertory are really amazing. One of them, apparently, enables you to survive for weeks without food; another will enable you to spend days in the snows of the Himalayas without suffering from the cold. At least, so I was told; I did not try them for myself, but I have no reason to doubt what I was told. I know that the power of herbs is quite extraordinary. There are books which tell of certain ointments or salves made of plant extracts, and with which witches in the Middle Ages smeared their bodies before taking part in the Sabbath. In point of fact, witches did not take part in a Sabbath in their physical bodies, but in their astral bodies. Some doctors, who have found some of the old recipes and experimented with them, have ascertained the authenticity of these phenomena. Of course, it is difficult to be sure that they have the exact formula of the ointments, because the indications are always somewhat distorted, but they all contained certain stimulants capable of inducing visions and astral projection.

But enough of this for the moment. My only purpose in talking about these things was to point out that these extremely potent substances do exist but that they are often extremely dangerous. For this reason I advise you never to use them on any pretext whatever. Fulfilment, freedom, spiritual buoyancy, joy and delight must be sought by purely spiritual means. This is the royal road. A true Initiate never relies on external props; he knows that God has placed all possibilities, all wealth and all the substances produced in laboratories within him. All he has to do is get them out and use them. Unfortunately, some people spend thirty, forty or fifty years in an Initiatic School without even beginning to learn how to exploit their inner resources? Why?

If you observe the behaviour of human beings, you will see that most of them have such an earthbound ideal that it prevents them from seeing, feeling or understanding reality. In fact, they instinctively reject the best and most useful things they may come across, because that is not what they are looking for: they have something else in mind. The secret, therefore, is to change one's ideal, to change one's goal in life. If your ideal is to become perfect, everything round you will contribute to enriching your life and giving you a true zest for reality. In this way the most ordinary activity of your daily life takes on extraordinary value and significance. But if your only ideal is to be rich, famous and influential on the physical plane, whatever you taste or experience in life will be insipid and unsatisfying. It does not matter if you are a professor, engineer, doctor, philosopher, artist, business man or Cabinet Minister: if you do not have the ideal of growing in perfection every day of your life, you will always lack the essential.

It is enough for me to see someone once, to know what his ideal is, and if it is divine, I can see his whole destiny laid out like a map before me. It is very simple for me, because I possess the true yardstick. Try to understand what I am saying: if your only ideal is to be successful in human society, you will always be deprived of what is essential. And what exactly is essential? It is the intimate conviction of being a child of God, the sense that Heaven and earth belong to you, the hope of a sublime future!

Each of our sense organs provides us with a partial knowledge of the world, and it is interesting to note the hierarchy that exists amongst them. The sense of touch is concerned principally with solids. One cannot feel gaseous or etheric matter at all and liquids only to a certain extent: the sense of touch really comes into its own when faced with solid, tangible realities. The sense of taste concerns liquids. If you object that a piece of toffee is solid enough, but that, when you put it into your mouth you can certainly taste that it is sweet, I would have to tell you that you have not studied the question fully: you can only taste what is in your mouth to the extent to which it has been melted and liquefied by saliva. And what about the sense of smell? This is what enables us to perceive odours, that is, gaseous emanations. So the nose is also concerned with matter. The sense of hearing, however, is no longer concerned with matter but with waves and vibrations. The same is true of the sense of sight: with sight we are at the threshold of the etheric world. So, you see, the senses are graded hierarchically, ranging from the physical to the etheric plane.

But now, if we want to penetrate into the astral world, we can no longer use our five senses. We need another sense specially adapted to perceiving even subtler forms of matter. Anyone who has not developed this sixth sense cannot even be aware that there are other levels of matter, other regions. He never imagines that the universe is threaded through and through with other vibrations which can provide sensations far vaster and more intense.

If we want to touch something we have to be very close to it; to taste something, even more so. We can smell the scent of a flower from a certain distance; we can hear sounds from quite far away, and we can see objects which are even farther away, for our eyes are designed to enable us to receive information and instructions from great distances. Here again, we see the marvellous intelligence with which nature has established this hierarchy amongst the five senses. And the sixth sense must now put us in touch with vaster, more remote and subtler regions of the universe.

But as long as our contemporaries (whether scientists, artists or spiritualists) have not developed the organs designed to put them in touch with more exalted entities in higher regions, their knowledge will be severely limited. They may talk, write, explain, criticize and pronounce judgment, but they will always be in error because they know only one aspect of reality. If they want to grasp the whole of reality they must practise until they succeed in awakening other faculties, faculties which have always been dormant within them and are only waiting to be used. In the far distant past, when man had not fully taken possession of his physical body, Initiatic tradition tells us that he lived mainly out of his body, in a state of astral projection. Later, when his spirit began to penetrate more deeply into matter, he developed the faculties which enabled him to work on the material level (the five senses) and neglected his mediumistic faculties. But he did not lose them altogether; he still possesses them.

Observe the attitude of children: up to the age of about seven they are still not wholly present in their physical bodies. They reflect the period during which humanity as a whole was at this stage of evolution. At that time men conversed with nature spirits and the souls of the dead, they were in touch and communicated with them, and when they themselves came to die they did not know whether they were alive or dead. The Invisible World, the spirit world, was the reality that was most apparent and most important to them. They floated in the atmosphere as though they were immaterial, and only entered their physical bodies every now and then. In these conditions they were totally unprepared to work in the material dimension. The evolutionary process, however, demanded that they penetrate this dimension. If science and technology have reached the heights we see today, it is thanks to this descent into matter: modern man is admirably equipped to dominate matter.

But in descending into matter, men forgot the very existence of the spiritual world; they completely lost touch with it; they forgot that they were immortal. Some, of course, still have some remembrance, an intuition of the spiritual dimension, but the majority has forgotten it.

Today, we are on the verge of a new cycle of evolution. I know the plans that Cosmic Intelligence has in mind, and I know that when human beings have learned to control and master matter and their own physical bodies, they will start to develop their spiritual senses and soar upwards again. You will say, 'If you know that, why are you always criticizing human beings and fulminating against them?' No, try to understand me: even if I have known for a very long time that this had to be, is that any reason not to urge those who are capable of doing so, to turn back at once to the Fountainhead? And the others? We'll just have to leave them behind! But don't worry about it: one day the whole of mankind will tread the path of spiritual ascension once again.

This is the answer for those who are fascinated by material reality and expect to find the solutions to all their problems by means of their five senses. Naturally, we must let our senses do their work; there is no question of chloroforming them! But to throw oneself headlong into the sensations provided by the physical body, in the hope of finding happiness, satisfaction and fulfilment, is to court disillusion. Those who want to advance and experience other, subtler, sensations, must start to reduce the sensations received through their five senses and look inwards. Their inner landscape is vast and very rich, but nobody ever looks there! Nobody even believes that there is anything to be found there. If God had not given me the grace of discovering these truths for myself, perhaps I, too, would have had great difficulty in believing them. But from my earliest youth I was privileged to experience the most extraordinary sensations. If, today, I can understand even the most obscure pages of Initiatic Science, it is because I have experienced them in my own life. If you have never experienced and tasted these things, you cannot understand, for they belong to another dimension.

Take, for example, the phenomenon of ecstasy. A great deal has been said and written about saints and mystics who had ecstasies. They never took any drugs, and yet they experienced the most extraordinary states, and those who met them were constantly amazed by what emanated from them. But, believe me: you cannot fake ecstasy! You can never make people believe that you have experienced ecstasy if your eyes don't express something luminous and divine. It is our eyes that are designed to express what we experience. If your eyes are dull, expressionless and lacklustre you have certainly not known ecstasy! When I was in India, I saw a disciple of Babaji who, supposedly entered the state of *samadhi*... Well, I was the only one who realized that, in fact, he was ill. When you have experienced ecstasy, you should be strengthened: your health and your inner light and intelligence should all be enhanced; if you are depressed or exhausted it was not ecstasy but a pathological condition. Ecstasy is an intense communion with the world of true reality; he who experiences it radiates light: his eyes are alight, his face glows with light! To be sure, certain experiences of this kind can tire the physical body, but a person's emanations cannot lie.

It is no good expecting the material world to give you anything that belongs to a higher dimension. I tell you categorically: you will never find it on this level. You can see proof of that in all those wealthy people who say, 'I have everything, and yet my life has no meaning!'

Many years ago, we bought a huge, tumbledown building for a song, and used the timber to build three or four cottages, and we engaged a carpenter, a Mr. Carrodano, and his sons to help us. At one point the father was working on the third chalet, the one near the path leading to the Rock[2], and every morning he would watch us coming down after the sunrise. One day, he said to me, 'Sir, I'm beginning to understand what you are doing here.' 'Ah, and what is that?' I asked. 'Yes, yes, I understand', he repeated. 'But what exactly do you understand, Mr. Carrodano?' I asked again. 'Well,' he said: 'I'll have to tell you about something that happened when I was very young, in Italy. I used to work with a whole team of youngsters like myself, and at lunch-time we all went to a run-down little restaurant, where we had macaroni and fried potatoes and a glass of wine. We were all carefree and full of fun, always laughing and joking. One day a gentleman came in; you could see that he was very rich from his clothes and his rings, but he had such a sad, gloomy face. He looked very unhappy. Well, this gentleman sat down and watched us. We were eating and drinking and laughing and playing the fool, as usual, you see, Sir.' 'Yes, yes. I understand, Mr. Carrodano.' 'Well, Sir, the man suddenly got up and came over to us, and he said: "Forgive me for interrupting you, my young friends, but I've been watching you, and you're so young and gay, it does me good to see you enjoying yourselves. You see, I'm very rich; I can have anything I want, but I'm not happy. Life has no meaning for me. But you are young and full of joy: will you do something for me? Will you order whatever you want to eat and drink, and I'll pay for it." Well, Sir, as you can imagine, we were delighted. We ordered ourselves a feast, and ate and drank to our heart's content! And he just sat there and watched us. Then he waved goodbye and left. And now, you see, I'm beginning to understand that that's what you're doing with your disciples: you're giving them the meaning of life.' 'Well done, Mr. Carrodano!' I said; 'But how did you discover that?' 'Ah, when I see them all coming down every morning, looking so shiny

---

[2] The Rock is a natural rocky plateau at the top of a hill near the Bonfin, to which the disciples go to meditate and watch the sunrise.

and joyful, I can see that that's what you're giving them: the meaning of life.' You cannot imagine how much pleasure his words gave me!

Of course, when you are young, it is normal to enjoy life, and to sing and be merry. But after a while, if you do not have a spiritual philosophy, vitality and youth are not enough. Youth is naturally happy; it does not need the help of philosophy or science or anything else to be happy. Yes, but as time goes on, the situation changes; you cannot count exclusively on your natural vitality and joy, they are not enough, you need a philosophy. Take the example of lovers: there they are, night and day, billing and cooing, but as often as not there is no mutual exchange on the level of ideas; the only kind of exchange between them is on the sexual and sentimental level. But after a while, feelings lose their edge, and then what is left? Each one feels the emptiness, the lack of intelligence or the absence of an ideal in their partner, and the misunderstandings and quarrels begin. And all because they had nothing in common on the intellectual and spiritual level. Yes, even where love is concerned, if you count only on the physical, sensual dimension, it will not last. Even lovers, who begin by devouring each other with their love, end by drifting apart if they have no common direction and no ideal.

In fact, this may surprise you, but if a young man and girl, who have no spontaneous liking or affection for each other, realize that they share the same philosophy and the same ideal in life, they will begin to appreciate and admire each other and they may well end by loving each other! So, you see, an ideal is extremely important, more important, perhaps, than all the sensations of the heart or sex.

For this reason, my advice to young people is this: 'Don't rely only on your youthful charms! Get a little philosophy into your heads as well!' Pretty legs and a pretty bosom are all very well, but men easily tire of even the prettiest things, and if a woman is empty-headed they will eventually leave her in the lurch! And the same applies to men. There are a lot of good-looking youngsters with elegant moustaches and nothing much in their heads, and when one of these whipper-snappers tells a girl that he will make her happy, he does not realize that what she most needs in order to make her happy is someone to guide and instruct and protect her. And as the poor wretch is, himself, in need of guidance and advice, she will soon leave him and look for someone else! And this is how so many tragedies happen. Believe me, my dear brothers and sisters; I have observed and analyzed so many situations, and had so much experience of life, that you can rely on what I say. If you don't believe me now, you will find out the truth for yourselves, one day; the trouble is, though, that it may be too late by then.

Accept the philosophy that the Initiates offer you, and you will no longer be like all those who search and search and never find. They spend their whole lives in a state of uncertainty and bewilderment, and yet they lack nothing. You may say that some people get along very well without philosophy or ideals or anything of the kind. I know; but it will not last: a few years from now their complacency will come to an end. At the moment they are perfectly happy because they are not sensitive to the spiritual dimension and are content with grosser satisfactions... like animals. Animals are perfectly happy because they don't need anything spiritual, so they are all right. Problems only arise when you start to move beyond the purely instinctive level: then you need something more; the things that made you happy before cannot satisfy you any longer. In spite of yourself, you begin to be harder to please, more discriminating, and, of course, you also begin to suffer, because your new needs make you acutely aware of your deficiencies. If you want to go on being perfectly happy on the physical level, whatever you do, don't advance spiritually; don't evolve! Continue to be like the stones, plants and animals! When you rise to the human condition, you can no longer be sure of being happy. The truth is that man can only find true happiness, constant, indestructible happiness by drawing constantly closer to the Godhead.

I assure you, as long as human beings continue to be nourished and moulded by the commonly accepted ideas of an undiscriminating public, they will never find contentment, the meaning of life or anything else. Whereas, if they seek the light of Initiatic Science, their consciousness will be most wonderfully illuminated! But one needs courage to do this. Very few dare to reject the ideas of the majority. It is safer to stick to the same dusty, well-worn tracks as everyone else, and this means that only a few adventurous individuals will be willing to adopt this new philosophy. But, I promise you, those who do, will discover the meaning of life and a new zest in the least little things. Whether they are working or resting, walking or talking, everything will be rich and significant to them. Otherwise, whatever they do in the attempt to enjoy life, they will always be dissatisfied and disappointed.

Some have already spoken to me about this: 'Master, it is becoming more and more obvious that love cannot be found on the physical plane. We have had several experiences of this nature, but we have not found the love we were looking for.' No, indeed! You cannot expect to find love by using your physical organs; you can use these organs in order to express love, but love itself has to be found elsewhere. But human beings need to experience disappointments and suffering in order to oblige them to realize that they must look for what they want on a higher level. If love were to be found on the physical level, everybody should have found it by now, since everybody 'makes' love! Besides, how do you explain the fact that physical love leaves many people unmoved and unsatisfied? Yes, why is this? A doctor would say that they were ill or abnormal. What an explanation!

So, to all of you who have come here for the first time, let me say this: 'Set aside all that you already know, all that you have read or heard! For just one month, ignore all that, and put a few rules of this Initiatic philosophy into your heads. Then, after a little while, look at yourself and see how you feel: you will find that you have begun to experience sensations that are quite new to you. For example, you stretch out on the ground, at night, to gaze at the stars: little by little, you are filled with a marvellous sensation of peace, a peace such as you have never known; you feel as though you were melting into the universe. And yet you have not had any alcohol or anything else! Or perhaps you are with the person you love, without speaking, without kissing; you are just together, and you feel filled with all the splendour of the universe!'

You must think about these things, therefore, and remember that if you repeated these experiences consciously, you would discover a world that is still unknown and unexplored. Unfortunately, people sometimes experience sensations like this once and then forget about them, as though they were chance accidents that happened for no known reason. Instead of exploring them in depth, they ignore them and set out, once more, on their quest for happiness. What a mistake! They should repeat the experience; they should say to themselves, 'It may be all an illusion, but I need that illusion because it gives me strength, intelligence and happiness, so I'm going to repeat it as often as possible.' And then they would find that this illusion leads them to reality.

Yes, this is how the Initiates discovered reality. They began by observing a sensation of fulfilment and expanded consciousness that was independent of their physical circumstances, and they endeavoured to recapture and amplify these sensations as often as possible. In this way, little by little, they became accustomed to living in the world of thought, a world of extremely tenuous, subtle matter. And this is what I advise you to do, too: if, at some point in your existence, you have had an instant of revelation, however short-lived, if you have already experienced a sensation of fulfilment, turn back to that moment, try to revive and relive it repeatedly, and you will see what progress it will help you to make. Most people are for ever replaying their old, negative recordings, in other words, they are capable of reviving only their experiences of anger, sorrow or discouragement. Don't be like the majority. You have those marvellous instants of the past still within you in the form of spiritual recordings, and you can constantly recall them and play them over and over again.

Now, let me add just a few words, in the hope of making this even clearer to you. We all know that a man is capable of succeeding in business and being at ease in society without prayer or meditation. Yes, but he will be blind to the subtle world. Whereas one who works on a spiritual level may not be so successful on the material level, but he will relish subtle elements which give him a joy that others, even though they possess everything, are incapable of! Of course, materialists will show off their houses, cars, businesses, etc., whereas spiritualists will be unable to show you anything of that kind. Generally speaking, people prefer what can be seen, but to my mind there is something seriously missing here, for what is visible is only half the picture. Those who work spiritually because of their high ideal will necessarily earn wealth that materialists will never have. The trouble is that they can never show you concrete evidence of that wealth. But it is real enough, concrete enough for them, since they are immersed in it, they live it. They cannot make a great show of it, but they live it. Whereas materialists can put everything they have on display, but they cannot live it. There is no more striking proof than life, nothing that speaks louder than to live the divine life. All the rest is the shell, the ashes, the outer surface of things.

We are constantly faced with the necessity of making a choice in life, and Initiates have always chosen life itself, for it is a million times better to possess life than to possess the whole world, if the world is dead. Initiates prefer to live, that is, to feel and taste life; whereas others prefer to be dead and to have great possessions. Well, I cannot say that that reveals great intelligence! The criterion of intelligence is to choose life, the subtlest, most intense form of life. This is how we evaluate intelligence in an Initiatic school. In the world, the evaluation of intelligence is based on a person's diplomas and worldly successes and even his possessions. But in the eyes of an Initiate, the most intelligent human beings are those who have chosen to live, to live with intensity; for life lived with intensity contains health, love, knowledge, light and power. Life contains it all.

Of course, when I speak of life, I am not speaking of biological, animal life, of mere vitality; all living creatures possess vitality. No, when I talk about life, I am talking about the spiritual life which is intelligence, light, love, kindness and joy. This is so clear to me! But how can I get human beings to understand it? How can I make it equally clear to them? They have been so badly educated. They always choose the heaviest, most cumbersome things, and in doing so they choose endless worry, because they live in terror of someone stealing their possessions! Oh, of course, I am not saying that you need no possessions, but I am saying that you should have only what you absolutely need, only as much as is necessary to give you the conditions you need to attain the subtle, intense life. As soon as you overstep the mark, possessions become a burden, a load that will weigh on you so heavily that you will no longer be able to rise to a higher plane and meditate and pray. Your thoughts will be stuck to that lifeless mass of material possessions and, in time, you too will be lifeless, you will be dead, stuck to all your wealth. Blessed are those who are content with the barest essentials and refuse to overload themselves!

When you meet people who are complacent about their great learning or wealth, take a good look at them and you will see that they are not happy: learning and wealth are incapable of making anyone happy. The education that men and women have been given has misled and deformed them, because it has never put them in touch with life, with divine life. And that is the only thing that we are trying to develop here, in our Teaching. But this requires an overwhelming love for the divine, luminous world, otherwise, during the short while that you are here, at the Bonfin, you will accept a little of what I tell you (barely five per cent) and, as soon as you get back home, your mystical and spiritual needs will fade out and you will start thinking and reacting, once again, like everybody else. I live in the world too, just like you, but the world's philosophy has no hold on me. This does not prevent me from loving human beings or from wanting to be of use to them, but I threw their philosophy overboard a very long time ago! Yes, I love human beings, but I am relentlessly opposed to their philosophy!

There, that is what I wanted to talk to you about today, about those inner senses that we all have, and that you must make up your minds to cultivate. Isn't this a fantastically convincing argument in favour of a spiritual philosophy? How else can you explain that a human being can experience very intense sensations and emotions without having eaten or drunk, breathed, heard or seen anything at all, if not by the fact that he has this inherent principle, capable of being stirred to life and vibrating in such a way as to give him sensations of extraordinary variety, strength and magnificence?

The Bonfin, 2 August 1969

Chapter Five

WHAT CAN WE LEARN
FROM A HOUSE?

For the last few days, you have been hard at work renovating this house and getting the whole property in order, and that is one thing you all know: that you must work. But the great question is how to work and what means and methods to use to do your work properly. I must say that not many people really know how to work! In fact, each one of you should ask himself, 'Am I working in accordance with the best rules and methods of this new Teaching?'

But before going on with the subject, I want to say a few words about the conference I went to the day before yesterday. It was a public conference on peace. There were several speakers, all highly qualified, intelligent, learned, and even amusing people. Thanks to them I learned that peace was something absolutely magnificent and the most desirable condition for humanity, whereas war was the worst possible scourge. I was truly delighted to hear this and I thought to myself, 'Ah, at last people are beginning to understand the advantages of peace. There is hope for mankind after all!'

However, I was anxious to hear how these people planned to bring about peace. Several speakers put forward some very intelligent plans, one of which was to form an international police force that would make it impossible for the different countries to fight each other. That is an excellent idea, but how could it be put into effect? How could you ever constitute an international police force with the integrity and impartiality necessary to fulfil such a function? It reminded me of the fable in which the mice convened a meeting to discuss how to defend themselves against the cat. They were sick to death of being chased and devoured by the cat, so they all put their heads together to see what they could do about it. After a great deal of discussion the senior mouse finally came up with the solution: the answer, he said, was to tie a bell round the cat's neck so that all the mice would hear it coming and have time to hide. You see how intelligent mice can be? They had realized that the cat always crept up on them so silently that they never heard it until it was too late! So this ingenious solution was agreed upon enthusiastically. Unfortunately, however, they never managed to find a mouse bold enough to go and tie the bell round the cat's neck! And it strikes me that the situation is exactly like that for this international police force!

Another speaker explained that federalism and pacifism were really the same thing, and he went on to discuss all kinds of complicated theories that nobody could quite follow. A third declared that the armed forces should all be done away with... without explaining how that was to be achieved. The story of the mice and the cat, once more! A fourth speaker spent his time denouncing the State for misusing the power invested in it to make slaves of its citizens. In the end, after listening to a great many speakers, I was forced to conclude that peace was not going to be established as soon as all that, for no one understood it or knew what it really was.

Peace is not a state that can be attained automatically, mechanically. If you seek peace and, at the same time, continue to entertain a murky, turbulent frame of mind, you will never find it. Peace is a result; it indicates a state of balance and harmony between all of man's internal and external functions and activities; it is a consequence of the correct organization and the perfect functioning of all his cells and organs. It is no good looking for peace on the outside: you will never find it. Since peace is a result, a consequence, we have to know the elements, means and methods to use in order to procure it, and this is a science in itself.

Let me give you a very simple example: take a man who has just eaten an enormous meal of sausages, ham and chicken, washed down with plentiful supplies of wine. Replete and satisfied, he says to himself, 'Ah, now for a quiet spot and a little rest,' and, finding just the place, he settles down for a nap. Before long he feels a certain queasiness inside, so he smokes a cigarette, and then he stretches and yawns and thinks, 'What I need now is a nice little woman...' Where can he find one? In his neighbour's house, of course. There is a wall round it but that is no obstacle; he leaps over the wall and... well, you can imagine the rest of the story for yourselves. But one thing is obvious: there can no longer be any question of peace! As long as man entertains lustful or envious desires, he will never find peace. In fact, we can say that peace is the result of a science which is very difficult to acquire and which only Initiates really possess.

In order to achieve peace, one must have a profound understanding of human beings and their complex psychic structure, with its different subtle bodies and the needs and aspirations of each one. In the meantime, one sees only rival factions bent on accusing each other of warmongering. For some, it is the rich who are to blame; for others it is the intelligentsia, politicians or scientists. Religious believers accuse the faithful of other Faiths of heresy and of leading humanity to damnation, and non-believers accuse believers of fanaticism. Look around you and you will see that everyone thinks that they can restore peace to the world by getting rid of some external, material factor, whether human or otherwise!

Not at all! Even if it were possible to get rid of armies and weapons, the very next day men would invent other ways of exterminating each other. Peace is an inner reality; it cannot be obtained simply by getting rid of externals. First and foremost we have to get rid of the causes of war within us. And in order to live in a state of inner peace, we have to learn how to behave on the three levels: mental, astral and physical.

Perhaps you will say that you can eat and drink whatever you like because your stomach never has the slightest problem: it can digest anything. That is possible, but it is still true that every time you eat or drink something impure, it contributes, however imperceptibly, to destroying your inner peace. Also, if you harbour sensual desires and appetites, your peace will vanish. You may try to cling to it, but you will not succeed, for by entertaining such desires you introduce the seeds of discord into your inner being.

Look at the reactions of a man who has committed a robbery: he is instinctively afraid that someone saw him and he cannot help imagining the awful consequences that might result: he is going to be followed, arrested and sent to prison! He can never be absolutely sure that he was not seen, that he did not leave some trace that would lead the police to suspect him or that he will not, one day, let slip something that will reveal where he has hidden the loot. He will never know a moment's peace again: he loses his appetite, suffers from insomnia and is obsessed by the need to hide. Or picture someone who has borrowed some money: he has promised to pay it back very quickly but, as time goes by and he does nothing about it, his creditors start to dun him and he is at his wit's end to know how to escape from them. Or take the case of a man who has spoken so harshly and unkindly to a friend that he has turned him into an enemy. Once again, peace has flown out of the window! Ah, yes: when it comes to losing his inner peace, man is highly talented! How could it be otherwise when he does not know the laws of justice, love, wisdom and purity?

Only the Initiates know what peace is. If peace is to reign on earth, the Initiates must come and establish their philosophy and carry out their own plans in the world. This is the only solution, and it is so simple that I don't quite know how to explain it to you! The great Masters are the only ones who are capable of restoring peace to the world. You will ask, 'But where are they, those Masters you talk about? Do they actually exist?' Yes, indeed they exist, but they will never impose themselves. Their teaching is a teaching of love and freedom, and they refuse to use the methods of the vulgar masses and resort to violence, or use their powers to command the elements to teach human beings a lesson. Initiates are capable of hurling thunderbolts and unleashing tornadoes and cyclones, of causing floods and earthquakes of such violence that they would destroy everything in their vicinity. Yes, they are capable of doing these things, but they have no desire to use their powers in that way.

Initiates are beings of extraordinary patience and love. In the past, it was they who governed and enlightened the nations, bringing them peace and prosperity. And later, when ambitious, violent creatures arose from the subterranean depths to sow the seeds of anarchy, the Initiates withdrew and left men to their own resources. But they are watching and waiting; watching the spectacle of ignorant philosophers and politicians groping in the dark and attempting to impose their own systems on the world. They know that no system of government created by those who look at things from below and from the outside will ever be truly beneficial and efficient.

The Initiates watch what is going on in the world, and when they see that men are beginning to tire of war and yearn sincerely for peace, perhaps, then, they will restore true authority to its rightful place in the world. True authority already exists in the universe: the authority, the supreme authority of the universe is God. The Angels and Archangels are God's servants who have the responsibility of seeing that His authority is respected, whereas the spirits of nature look after the equitable distribution and sharing of nature's riches. When the Initiates come back, they will establish an organization on earth modelled on that of Heaven, and it is they who will wield authority. For the Initiates are God's representatives on earth, they are in constant communication with the Lord, and when they hold counsel together, they always consult His opinions, His wishes and plans. And they will transmit the divine decrees to the kings and representatives of the people, so that all their acts of government faithfully reflect God's plan and put it into effect. Finally, they will name an economic council to organize the production and distribution of wealth. This is the type of government that the Initiates will establish on earth when men are finally tired of suffering, tired of always being at odds, of always massacring each other. For the moment, everyone has his own opinion: 'I say we should do this... I say we must do that...' Everybody has a different opinion and, as everybody wants to impose their own point of view, the result is perpetual strife!

There is only one way to straighten out the situation, and that is to call on the Initiates to come and take charge. And the day this happens, the day they respond to our call, you will see how wonderfully they will improve the situation! If we trust them, if we say to them: 'We trust you absolutely and put all our faith in you. Guide us and teach us. You are the only ones who can give us the knowledge we need to rebuild our lives', they will see our sincerity and willingness to obey and cooperate with them, and they will agree to help us. And, as they are clairvoyant, they will say, 'In such and such a town there is a man of very modest means who is almost unknown, but he is the greatest judge you could find. Go and fetch him!... The greatest doctor in the world lives in such and such a village...' In this way, they will find and assemble all those who are destined to be the leaders of the future. Then the entire world will enjoy prosperity because, when the Initiates have found those who are best qualified in each country, they will tell the

What Can We Learn From a House?

people: 'These are the men who will be your link with the Godhead. Listen to them, for the Spirit of God is upon them. They will lead you on the path of progress, peace and happiness.'

The Initiates are perfectly capable of ruling the earth at once, today, but they are waiting, for there are still too many ambitious, grasping human beings who have no intention of making way for them. Don't think that the violent, the rapacious, the connivers are eager to give up what they have got! But it is up to the population as a whole to understand and clamour vociferously and in the greatest possible numbers for the Initiates to come and help us. When they come, they will get rid of all those who are useless and worse than useless. But before that day comes, of course, the world is still going to have to experience all manner of tribulations.

Now, let's go back to the subject of a house. As I was saying, you work hard every day, building it, but you have never reflected on all the profound lessons it has to offer. You think, 'Why it's just a house! What's so special about a house?' Well, of course, everyone has seen plenty of houses. But who ever remembers that everything that surrounds us, all the things we need in life, everything we do has deep significance? This is what I mean by the great book of nature. Our gestures and habits contain all that is contained in Esoteric Science, but we have to learn to decipher them; we have to have eyes that are capable of seeing and reading them.

When you intend to build a house, what is the first thing you do? You draw a design, a plan, don't you? The plan of your house begins its existence as an idea, on the invisible plane, before it, is put down on paper, that is, on the physical, visible plane. Once your drawings are complete, you start collecting all the materials you need, and, finally, you hire some workmen to come and put your plan into execution. So there are three distinct phases: preparing the plans, collecting the materials and building.

And once you are ready to build, where do you begin? With the roof? No, of course not! You begin with the base, the foundations. You think that this is obvious, don't you? Well, it is not as obvious as all that; in fact, for some people it is very far from obvious! As it happens, very few have understood. Once the foundations are in place, you proceed with the walls and, finally, the roof. For the external shell of a house, therefore, you work from the bottom up. But what about the interior? Do you start by polishing the floor? No. You start with the ceiling, next you do the walls, and the floor comes last. So, on the inside of a house you work from the top down. And finally, when all the building is done, you take care of the aesthetic aspect: decoration, paintings on the walls, curtains in the windows, and so on.

On the exterior, therefore, we work from bottom to top, and on the interior, we work from top to bottom. And from this we see that a house teaches us how to work with the two currents of evolution and involution. All the work involved in building and decorating a house is summed up and symbolized by the two intertwined triangles which make up the Seal of Solomon. This symbol, the Seal of Solomon, contains a world of science. It reveals how God created the world and also how we, ourselves, should work. One of the first lessons to be learned from it is that the methods we use in our outer life should not be the same as those we use in our inner life: when we work on the physical plane we should work from the bottom up, whereas in our inner life, we must begin at the top and work down to the bottom. I can see that you find this surprising! But there is really no cause for astonishment. If you want to succeed in the physical world, you must work in accordance with the laws of evolution and begin with the solid, material dimension, and gradually work up to subtler dimensions. When you have some work to do on the psychic, inner level, on the other hand, you must begin at the top, that is, you must begin with what is divine, with the subtlest, most luminous aspect, and end with the concrete realization on the visible level. But how many have learned to work in this way? Everybody knows how to build a house, to be sure, but when it comes to applying the same rules to one's own existence that is another matter!

If you want to get results in the material world, you have to begin by laying a firm, solid foundation. Whereas, to get results in the spiritual world, you must first of all be sure that you have a good, solid roof over your head, otherwise even your foundations will crumble. Yes, for in the inner world of the spiritual life, everything is reversed; it is as though the foundations were at the top and the roof at the bottom. This means that you must build things in your mind, first of all, before trying to achieve them on the physical plane, and, as it takes a very, very long time for spiritual constructions to reach the physical plane, you are going to have to work at them for years, if you want them to become concrete reality one day.

The downward movement, from top to bottom, teaches us how God created the world. In order to create, God had to manifest Himself, that is, He had to go out of Himself, as it were and 'descend' into matter. But this first downward movement, which we call involution, is followed by an upward movement, in the course of which God goes back into Himself. And this is what we call evolution. In a first movement God goes out from Himself to create, then He turns back into Himself and reintegrates creation into Himself. But these two movements take billions of years to accomplish.

The involutionary movement flows from top to bottom (or from the centre to the periphery) whereas the evolutionary movement rises from the bottom to the top (or from the periphery to the centre). Involution precedes evolution; it is a process of materialization, whereas evolution, on the contrary, is a process of dematerialization. In nature, both movements are constantly being produced and constantly encountering and interacting with each other, and it is this interaction that gives birth to life in all its forms. New forms are ceaselessly being created in space, by the interaction of these two movements, which are the movements of God Himself. It is not a question, here, of spirit as opposed to matter; it is life, only life, that flows ceaselessly between the top and the bottom, the centre and the periphery. Forms become more and more subtle as they approach the centre, and more and more solid and material, as they move away from the centre towards the periphery. All these forms flow through creation, therefore, some becoming gradually more subtle and others more material.

These two processes of evolution and involution can be seen, also, in our lives. The birth of a child is an involutionary movement: it is a descent into matter; but when a man dies, it is an evolutionary movement: he disengages himself from matter and turns back to the spirit. Similarly, to undress is an evolutionary movement, and to dress is an involution. And even in the different gestures we make while dressing, we can see the two patterns of evolution and involution: some clothes have to be stepped into and pulled up from below; others have to be pulled down from the top. But has anyone ever noticed and reflected on these things?

It is the interaction of these two currents that formed man. To begin with, man was a head, nothing more. It was only a great deal later that the heart, lungs and stomach, etc. were gradually added. At that time, man was still invisible; his head was like a ball of fire floating on the etheric plane, and he began to materialize on the physical plane only when his feet had finally been formed. First his feet, and then his legs, thighs, genital organs, solar plexus and stomach and so on, gradually solidified, all the way up to his head. His head, therefore, was the last part of man's body to be materialized, although it was the first to be formed; and his feet, which were formed last, were materialized first. But I expect all that is rather difficult for you to imagine or understand!

The two currents of evolution and involution are also to be found in astrology. If you read the signs of the Zodiac beginning with Aries and going on to Taurus, Gemini and Cancer, etc., you are following the involutionary movement. This is the order in which man was formed on the subtle planes of being, starting with Aries, the head, for, as you know, each sign of the Zodiac corresponds to a particular part of the human body. But the Vernal point moves in the opposite direction: Pisces, Aquarius, Capricorn, Sagittarius, Scorpio, etc. Its movement follows the evolutionary order, which was the order in which man's physical body materialized. And if we look at the movement of the Zodiac in relation to that of the planets, we find the same opposition. The constellations rise in the heavens in the order of Aries, Taurus, Gemini etc., whereas the planets move in the opposite direction. The movement of the planets is involutionary, therefore, and that of the constellations evolutionary.

The opposition between the planets and the Zodiac can also be studied from another point of view. The Zodiac represents stability, immutability. In contrast to the planets which are constantly moving, the signs of the Zodiac are always in the same place and the same order. Aries never rubs shoulders with Libra; Pisces has never been known to slip between Leo and Virgo. The constellations have kept to the same order from all eternity, whereas the planets are never in the same place or in the same order in relation to each other from one day to the next. By contrast with the physical dimension which is permanent and stable, they represent the psychic dimension which is constantly shifting and changing. Our head, stomach and feet are always in the same place! Each organ and each member, just like each sign of the Zodiac, is in the position assigned to it from the beginning of creation. Whereas, inside the body, everything is in a state of mobility and flux: the blood, humours and nervous currents flowing ceaselessly through the organism and reflecting the ceaseless motion of the planets.

On the other hand, we know that the characteristics of a planet will be enhanced or, on the contrary, debilitated, by the sign in which it finds itself at any given moment, and that, at the same time, it exerts its own influence on that sign. When Mars is in Aries, for instance, he is strong and forceful, because Mars and Aries are strongly compatible; they understand and draw strength from each other. But when Mars reaches another sign, Cancer or Libra, for example, he loses much of his strength, because these signs are foreign to him. Similarly, those elements within us which represent the planets, our forces and feelings, are exalted or debilitated depending on the organ or centre through which they manifest themselves. If your love is in your head it will not behave in exactly the same way as if it were in your heart. And if you put your wisdom somewhere other than in your brain, what effect will it have? It is only when forces and organs are compatible and in sympathy with each other that they enhance and draw energy from each other. Astrologers have never studied these aspects: just as the planets are exalted or in fall in certain signs, in the same way, our qualities and virtues, our passions and feelings, are stronger or weaker depending on the organs through which they pass and manifest themselves.

But I don't want to linger on the subject of astrology: let's get back to the symbolism of a house. The thing to remember, above all, is that if you want to succeed in the psychic, spiritual world, you must begin by building the roof, followed by the walls and, finally, the foundations. Yes, because, in the spiritual world, the roof is the base, the foundation, the ground on which we must build... But, to avoid confusion, I shall continue to call it the roof. When I say, therefore, that if you want to build something on the spiritual level you have to begin by building the roof, this means – amongst other things – that before assuming the role of a sage, prophet, clairvoyant or healer, you must study for a long time, and be in close contact with the Lord, so as to be strongly rooted in the divine world. You have to study and build patiently for years before your spiritual work can begin to be reflected on the physical plane. Very often, people do just the opposite: as soon as they embark on the spiritual life, they want everybody to know about it! No, the truth is that the results of your labours will become visible only after years and years of meditation and prayer. Work and pray and leave things to show up on the visible plane when they are ready to do so! When the time comes, there will be no need for words, in fact; what you are will be made manifest even in spite of yourself.

Let the Invisible World reveal itself visibly in your facial expression, your eyes, your voice, your gestures. Some people come and confide in me that they are Jesus, Napoleon or the Blessed Virgin! In fact I had a letter, one day, which said, 'The Heart of the Integral Universe greets you. It was very touched by this or that...' Naturally, I was flattered to be honoured by such a letter, but there you have someone who has not understood the construction of a house. Even if you are a saint, a divinity, you must not talk about it; it must become apparent all by itself; it must be felt and revealed by other people. This is how a genuine Initiate functions. He builds in silence, on the invisible level, for years, and, one day, even the blindest of the blind begin to notice and exclaim, 'Oh, but there is a building here!' But if you try to convince people that you are the Heavenly Father or the Virgin Mother, they will lock you up, just as they would lock up anyone who tried to put up the roof of his house before laying the foundations! If you tell others, 'I'm very rich, very powerful and very intelligent', they will reply, 'Prove it! Let's see what you have accomplished so far.' They will never take your word for it: they will want tangible proof. If you cannot show them your wealth and power they will refuse to believe you: it will be no good pointing to something that you have only just begun to construct. And this holds true in the spiritual life as well, with the difference that those who are perfectly capable of appreciating your achievements on the physical plane, are far less perceptive on the spiritual plane. In other words, you are going to have to work for a long, long time.

They have a tale, in Bulgaria, about a young peasant who

married a very tall girl from another village. After the wedding the nuptial procession went to the bridegroom's house, and the bride was so tall and stiff that she could not get through the door without bending... but she was much too proud to bend! What could be done? The boy's parents puzzled about it for a while and then decided that there were only two possible solutions: either they could pull down the front of the house and make a bigger door, or they could cut off the bride's head! What a quandary! But this is how people often behave in life: they refuse to climb down, to humble themselves or give in, with the result that heads roll or houses are demolished! Isn't it true that people often tear down their house rather then humiliate themselves by giving in? Two young people want to get married and, one fine day, there they are, in front of the magistrate or the priest... and then, not long after, as neither of them is willing to 'bend' a little, they end by tearing down the house. The only solution would have been to have a little more humility, then both of them would have been able to enter the house.

I know that you are all thinking, 'Fortunately that story doesn't concern me!' Doesn't it? What about when you argue with someone and refuse to admit their point of view? You lose your temper and fly into a rage, and in this way you waste all your energy and spend the rest of the day in a state of nervous prostration, utterly demagnetized. Wouldn't it have been much more sensible to give way? If you had humbled yourself a little you would have saved your strength, your inner 'house'. You should have said to yourself, 'I shall gain more from giving in. I must learn to be more patient, more tolerant and loving!' When I say you should learn to give in, I am saying that you should be more intelligent and tactful, gentler and humbler and more understanding; I am not recommending that you say 'Amen' to every idiotic or unjust demand.

When I came in this morning, I saw that you had cleaned the floor before you had finished painting the walls. That proves that you don't use your brains very much. Why do you think God gave you a brain? Every one of you would assure me that you are full of good will. I know, and that is magnificent, but it is not enough. When you begin any type of work, you must always take a certain number of rules into account: that a certain order and sequence must be respected, for instance, or that you must clean your tools when you have finished with them. If you work in a clean room with dirty tools, you will only make things dirty and have to clean up all over again, and that is not very intelligent! You will say that it is not important, that you have a Ph.D in Science! That may be, but everything is interconnected, and from the way in which someone works on the physical level, I can tell exactly how he works on the intellectual and spiritual level and to what extent he is going to succeed in life; I can tell him what his future holds, all the difficulties and complications that are in store for him, and all the dangers to which he will be exposed. By seeing how fast or how slowly he works, or how he handles his paint brush, in fact, I can even tell him how strong his nervous system is! Yes, for the whole person is reflected in everything one does on the material level. The material world is a building site on which we have to work and practise until we are proficient and capable of accomplishing something on the spiritual level.

You must realize, also, that whatever work you have been given to do by Providence or destiny, you must do it perfectly. This is how you climb the ladder of evolution; whereas if you say to yourself, 'I can't be bothered to do this job properly; it is beneath me. I deserve better than that!' you will cease to evolve and, later on, you will be obliged to come back to correct and repair your errors and repeat your lessons. When this happens, you will realize how difficult it is to begin a job all over again when you thought that you had finished it already. If we are here, on earth, at this very moment, and have so many difficulties to contend with, it is precisely because we are repeating something that we have already done... and done badly. We have been sent back here in order to recognize that we don't know how to work and that we must learn. If we refuse to learn, we are going to be sent back again and again, and it will become more and more difficult to correct our mistakes. By their ignorance of the reality of reincarnation and the reason for it, human beings make it impossible for themselves to follow the path of evolution.

If you only knew what profound science is concealed in each gesture that you make when you are working! Even though this work is, apparently, the least spiritual thing you could be doing, the whole universe is reflected in your gestures. When you are renovating a room, you have to follow a certain order: the ceiling, the walls (including the doors and windows) and, lastly, the floor. And it is exactly the same in your inner, psychic life. You must begin by thinking (the ceiling); symbolically speaking, you hang up your lamps and switch them on so as to have light. Secondly you feel that what you propose to do is good. And, finally, you do it. When the time comes to act you do not walk about on the walls or the ceiling, but on the floor. The ceiling, walls and floor correspond to the three dimensions of thought, feelings and action. Light, that is to say, wisdom, intelligence and knowledge, comes from above; the dimension of feelings is the walls on which you hang pictures, mirrors and all kinds of beautiful things, and the dimension of action is the floor, the ground on which you walk or stand and work. The windows are your eyes; this is why we have to wash our windows, so as to be able to see clearly. There: this is what I mean by the Book of Living Nature. You will never come to the end of all the lessons in this Book.

A lot of people begin with the floor, that is, by acting. They act first; and they are very busy, getting things done and bustling about in all directions until, inevitably, they begin to suffer and realize that something is wrong. Only then do they pause to reflect and draw conclusions. But that is what they should have

What Can We Learn From a House?

done to begin with! Often enough, people think that it would be a good idea to try things out first, and to draw conclusions afterwards. No, it is much better to begin by reflecting and preparing a plan of action. This is all very simple and clear. Everything around us is a magnificent book... but we forget to read it! Now, after this, I shall be watching to see how you apply these rules!

Remember, especially, that on the physical level, you must work according to the evolutionary movement whereas, on the spiritual level, you must work according to the involutionary method, the method of the spirit. When a man shows off his cars and houses and university degrees to a woman, she immediately feels that she can trust him. When a customer goes to buy something in a shop, the shopkeeper is interested not in whether he is kind and intelligent, but in whether he is going to pull out his wallet, and whether he has plenty of money in it! But where Heaven is concerned, the situation is quite different: you can try to make an impression by spreading out all your material belongings, but if that is all you have, you will simply be told: 'We don't know you. You haven't begun to build your roof up here yet.' However powerful and wealthy, and however highly respected a man may be in the physical world, he will never be loved and respected and sought after on high, until he begins to cultivate the virtues and pure and noble thoughts.

Anyone who thinks that, just because he has succeeded in the material world, he is sure to succeed in the spiritual world, is mistaken. They are two quite distinct domains. Similarly, anyone who thinks that, because he has begun to develop his virtues and qualities, he will necessarily succeed in the physical world, is equally mistaken. His virtues are not very visible, and materialists have no respect for them. If you want to be understood and appreciated on the physical plane, you must work with the methods used by the evolutionary currents, that is, start by laying firm foundations here, on earth. Whereas, if you want to succeed on the invisible level, if you want to be welcomed and protected by heavenly spirits and enjoy revelations, ecstasies and fulfilment, you have to work with the methods of the involutionary current, that is, begin by putting down roots in Heaven. The best solution, obviously, is to work with both currents, so as to be well received by both Heaven and earth; Heaven will recognize you as an Initiate and men will recognize you as someone who is capable of getting things done on earth.

There is no room in our school for visionaries who want everybody to adopt their own cranky ideas. What we need are people who can contribute luminous, sensible ideas and who are capable of doing some good, clean, solid work on the material level. Unfortunately people like that are not in the majority, today! Most people are either highly qualified on the physical level and ignorant of spiritual things, or spiritualists who walk around with their 'roofs' in the clouds and are incapable of achieving anything concrete. True disciples of an Initiatic school must learn the laws of the spiritual world and start by putting their spiritual house on solid foundations, while, at the same time, learning to manifest themselves on the physical level through their work and their sensible behaviour. In this way they will be perfect, well balanced beings in both worlds.

There: that is what we can learn from a house.

Why do you think I told you to begin by renovating the inside of the house first? In order to show you that you must always begin by cleansing and purifying your own interior. It is symbolic. This purification will reflect on you; it will show in your eyes, your complexion, your gestures. In the meantime, don't try and make yourself out to be anything special, for you will only make yourself ridiculous! Let things manifest themselves in their own way and their own time; the only thing that matters for you is to work. As you know, I have never claimed to be an Initiate, a prophet or a clairvoyant! I simply said that I was continuing the Master Peter Deunov's work; I did not even say that, until years and years after he had given me my mission.

The day before yesterday, in the hope of getting you to work faster, I told you that we would consecrate the house today... but it is not finished yet. The building site you are working on is that of the Brotherhood and the way you work is being observed from on high. It is important that you realize that every time you do some cleaning on the outer dimension, you are also cleaning yourself inwardly and every time you make something more beautiful outwardly, you are making yourself more beautiful inwardly.

As you can see, my dear brothers and sisters, it is not to the advantage of human beings to maintain the present disorder in the world. It is not to their advantage to continue to suffer for no other reason than their lack of light and love and the ambitions of a few cruel, evil, egotistical people. On the contrary, it is very much to their advantage to live in joy, freedom and fulfilment. This is why they should implore Heaven to bring all the Initiates in the world together to help them, for they, at least, are disinterested; they have no desire to mislead or enslave anyone; on the contrary, it is they who will restore the Golden Age in the world – as they did once before in the past – and then life will blossom and flourish once again. You must beg and implore the Initiates to come. Do this inwardly. There will be no solutions forthcoming from those who understand neither human beings, nor nature, nor the laws, virtues and forces, nor the Angelic Hierarchies. Whatever system they propose will turn out to be ineffectual. Only Initiates are capable of bringing mankind the blessings it yearns for.

Sèvres, 6 July 1947

Chapter Six

HOW THOUGHT IS MATERIALIZED ON THE PHYSICAL PLANE

We have often talked about the problem of thought: what thought is, how it works, how it materializes on the physical level and the conditions it needs in order to do so. But I sense that we need to talk about it again, for a great many things in your lives depend on how well you understand this question. Many of your problems will remain unsolved if it is not clear in your minds.

Certain spiritualists who read that thought is an all-powerful force, instantly start to practise mental concentration in the hopes of getting results on the physical plane. But the trouble is that they don't take the time to study the question properly beforehand and find out when this is true and when it is not. And if they don't understand the question correctly, they can concentrate for years on end but they will never get any results! It is true that thought is all-powerful, but we have to begin by knowing what it is, in what regions and with what materials it works and how its influence works progressively through the successive layers of reality until it reaches the material world.

Nature has subjected the universe to certain laws: why do men waste so much time and energy trying to thwart those laws? If you want to get a lump of sugar to jump out of the sugar bowl into your mouth, you can concentrate for all you are worth, but it won't happen, and you will be discouraged and disappointed. Whereas, all you have to do is stretch out your hand, pick up a lump of sugar and pop it into your mouth: no fuss or bother! Nature gave us hands with which to pick things up. You will say, 'But then, what can one do with thought?' With thought you can do far more important things than that, but you must know its nature and its mechanism; you must know how it works.

Thought is a force, an energy, but it is also an extremely subtle matter which operates in a remote region, far removed from the physical plane. Take the example of radio and television antennae: you have all seen different kinds of antennae on the roofs of houses or on top of a tower, and you know that they are used to pick up waves, vibrations. But do they pick up something material? Have they accumulated some particles of all that they pick up over the years? No, their weight and volume are still the same: they have been receiving something, but that something is not material. There always has to be a physical, material point of departure to produce waves, but the waves themselves are not material. So, antennae pick up certain vibrations and wavelengths, and transmit them to various instruments, and these instruments, in turn, transmit them to others, thereby triggering physical phenomena.

All the secrets of nature are there, before our eyes, but we don't see or understand them. Take the example of a ball: if I kick a ball or hit it with a bat, I am giving it energy. I am not adding anything material to it, but it is set in motion by the energy I have transmitted to it and it will continue to move until that energy has all been used up or an obstacle gets in its way. These two examples, the antennae and the ball, help us to understand that the thoughts we formulate do not touch the visible, dense layers of matter; they only touch and transmit vibrations to that which is similar to themselves, to the subtlest

How Thought is Materialized on the Physical Plane

elements that exist in ourselves and others. Yes, thought communicates itself in exactly the same way as kinetic energy communicates itself to a ball.

Thought as energy, force or vibration is picked up by the antennae connected to certain centres in our bodies. When these antennae, which are located in the brain or on an even higher level, in the etheric region, start to vibrate, they transmit messages to other instruments and various effects are set in motion in our physical body: recordings are made, energies, forces and even chemical substances start to circulate. None of this is visible, of course; it would be useless to try to see the effects on the physical plane. But something happens on the subtle plane and, if you do what needs to be done to pass on this communication to other, less subtle regions and less refined instruments, you can completely restore the whole system of contacts and communications. A human being is like a factory, fully equipped with machines and instruments of all kinds; all the tubing and cables are in place; the only thing that remains to set it all in motion is to push one little button that is connected to an electrical circuit which, in turn, is connected to a series of cog-wheels and transmission belts; as soon as you push it, all the machines start functioning.

Similarly, in nature, everything is interconnected, so that, if you manage to set up an analogous series of connections within yourself, your thought can produce tangible results on the physical plane immediately. But if the channels of communication are not properly connected from one level to another, your thought cannot be effective: there will be gaps, dead zones where the current cannot get through. The great question is to know how to restore the connection. In a factory, when one link in a production line is missing (a broken transmission belt, a gear wheel that loses some teeth and fails to move the wheel next to it, a small wire that has been accidentally cut), communication is interrupted. And the same thing happens with thought.

When you form a thought, it produces an effect in its own region and sets in motion very subtle instruments; but nothing can happen on the physical plane until the lines of communication are open. As soon as communication has been established, the energies are free to circulate and produce material results. When this is the case, thought becomes truly powerful, truly magic.

Now, let's try to make this completely clear: it is absolutely true to say that thought is powerful and that it always materializes, but you have to understand how this happens. Take the example of a man who becomes a thief. To begin with he does not dare to go further than the simple thought: 'Aha, there's no one about; I could easily slip in and take that. Life would be much simpler if I had that...' He still has no real desire or intention to do so but, from time to time he continues to think about it and to picture the scene in his mind: he sees the crowds in the streets and shops and imagines himself slipping his hand into someone's pocket or purse or snatching something from a shop counter. All this is on the mental level; he is still incapable of actually doing anything. But the thing is that, as his thoughts are all being recorded, they set certain wheels in motion on the astral plane and, from there, they soon move down onto the level of matter. And, for the thief, the realization of his thought on the level of matter means the gesture, the concrete application, the actual theft. To begin with, it was as though nothing were happening at all; nothing could be seen of what this man was plotting: outwardly he seemed perfectly honest. But his thoughts had already reached the level of feeling; he had already begun to wish with all his might for their realization, and from there to the material gesture is only a short step. The lines of communication are in place, the connections are already being made without his realizing it and, one fine day, his hand simply reaches out and takes somebody's wallet or a valuable object. It is clear, isn't it? His thought, which began by being high up on the mental plane, descended onto the astral plane, the plane of desire, and, from there, onto the physical plane. How can you continue to believe that thought is not effective on the material plane? The effects of that man's thought are considerable: he could become very rich or he could end up in prison!

Take another example: that of a very gentle, idealistic, easy-going man; he is so mild that if someone struck him, he would turn the other cheek! But then, one day, he starts reading historical books and begins to be fascinated by certain thinkers or statesmen whose speeches and actions revolutionized society and led the masses into all kinds of adventures. He becomes passionately absorbed in the story of their lives, reads nothing but their writings, and begins to be very bold and adventurous himself. To start with he is content to discuss his ideas with others; then he feels the need to act, so he joins a political party, discovers that he is capable of swaying a crowd and ends by leading a revolution in his country. How can you deny that thought is extraordinarily powerful? It is invisible, it cannot move a lump of sugar, but when it materializes on the physical plane, it can change the face of the world! The only thing is that one has to understand how and under what conditions it is powerful. It is ridiculous to think that thought can act directly on matter without passing through the different levels of reality. The mental and physical worlds are so different and so far from each other: direct contact is impossible.

Thought can pass through walls and physical objects without a trace; in order to get it to take effect on the material level, you have to build bridges, that is to say, a series of intermediaries. Send it through these intermediaries and you will see that it is capable of shaking the universe to its foundations. This is the meaning of that famous saying of Archimedes: 'Give me a lever and I will move the earth!' Archimedes meant that he could not act directly on the world: he needed an intermediary: the lever. An intermediary is always necessary. Thought is powerful and effective on condition that we pass it through the intermediaries that allow it to descend all the way to the level of matter. This is why I have been talking to you about this question for years.

You all have wonderful, divine ideas, I know; but what results have they produced? None? That proves that you still have some work to do to bring your ideas down onto the physical plane. Yes, that is the important thing: to get them to descend into matter. You say, 'I have an idea!' Well done! Good for you! But your idea will leave you to die of hunger and thirst if you don't know how to bring it down to the level of your heart and, from there, materialize it in acts. It is not enough to have ideas. A great many people have ideas, but they live in such a way that there is never any connection between their ideas, their feelings and their actions. There must be a link, a means of communication, a bridge; the current must be switched on. Thought cannot make direct contact with matter; it needs the intermediary of feeling before it can touch and transform matter. An idea only takes on flesh and blood and becomes capable of influencing matter when it enters the dimension of the emotions.

Feeling, therefore, is the lever that is capable of touching matter. Thought is too remote, too subtle; it passes through matter without touching it or causing it to vibrate. It can only touch our 'antennae', the subtlest of our instruments which exist on a very high level, in the domain of the spirit. In order to reach the level of matter, the spirit has to pass through the soul, that is to say, through the mind and the heart. Let me explain this to you by analogy, with the help of a phenomenon familiar to all of you: the action of the sun on air, water and earth.

The sun heats the air and water vapour contained in the atmosphere and, when the air is warm, it tends to rise, thereby creating zones of low pressure, whereas the colder air is compressed as it is forced down to the ground, thus creating zones of high pressure. Winds are created by the movement of air from the zones of high pressure towards the zones of low pressure and, when the difference in pressure becomes very great, the winds become stronger and more violent, sometimes producing devastating tornadoes and hurricanes. The sun also heats the water of oceans, seas, lakes and rivers, and turns it into water vapour which rises into the air. When the air reaches the point of saturation, all that water vapour is transformed into rain or snow and then showers and storms act on the earth, creating the contours of hills and valleys. Day after day, these atmospheric phenomena occur over the whole surface of the earth, and it is the sun that causes them.

In man, the sun corresponds to the spirit, air to the mental body, water to the astral body, to feelings, and the earth to the physical body. When the spirit acts on thought, thought, in turn, acts on the feelings, and the feelings surge into the physical body, causing it to move, to make a gesture, to speak. The physical body, therefore, is moved by feeling, feeling is aroused by thought and thought is born through the influence of the spirit.

This mechanism is there, before our eyes, every day: under the influence of air, water acts to model the earth, to sculpture it and give it form. Hollow areas are filled with alluvial deposits, hillsides and cliffs erode and slide into the sea, and so on. In the same way, man can act on his own physical body, on condition that he uses air and water as his intermediaries. And, in this case, air represents the nervous system and water represents the blood. The nervous system regulates the circulation of the blood in our bodies, and the blood deposits certain elements and washes away others, thus modelling the physical body.

We could study this image of how the sun influences nature in much greater detail, but there is no point in doing so. It is the general idea that interests me, and that idea is that, if human beings knew how to interpret and apply to their inner lives, this normal, natural process of the sun's action on the earth through the intermediary of air and water, they would be capable of tremendous transformations, both inwardly and outwardly. This is what the power of thought consists of! The most important thing to realize is that thought cannot exert its influence directly on the physical plane. We don't pick up burning coals with our hands: we use tongs. And we don't help ourselves to soup with our hands, either, we use a ladle. And the pattern is the same in every domain. Do you want to know what an arm is, for instance? An arm is the intermediary between a thought and an object. When I pick up a lump of sugar, who is actually performing the action? My thought. Yes, through the arm that serves as its intermediary, it is my thought that acts. And suppose my thought remains inactive; what then? I still have an arm, but if there is no thought and no desire to stimulate it to take a lump of sugar, it will not do so. It is in this sense that one can speak of the power of thought.

It is always thought that urges men forward or holds them back, it is thought that gives rise equally to war and devastation or to the noblest endeavours. Yes, it is thought that does everything, but only on condition that it has an arm with which to work concretely. And man is also an executor, an arm. Man's arm is a symbol of the whole man, and man himself is the symbol of a cosmic arm. Yes, a man's arm represents the whole man; man himself is an arm for thought, and your thought can be an arm for yet other thoughts which exist on a much higher plane, and so on, all the way to the Deity, who uses all the arms of the universe, that is to say: all creatures.

You can see, now, why Initiatic Science has always taught that all the things we see in nature: animals, insects, trees, mountains, lakes, fruit and flowers... all these things are crystallized thoughts. Yes, everything is a thought that was originally projected by God and has become visible. You too: you are all thoughts that have materialized. Man is a thought, an idea. In fact, if you want to know what kind of thought or idea gave rise to a particular creature, it is sufficient to see the form that it has taken. If a creature is perfect, it means that the thought that gave birth to it was perfect. Every thought materializes: an octopus, a worm, a scorpion and a tiger have all taken on the

How Thought is Materialized on the Physical Plane

colour, shape and general appearance of the thought that dwells in them: a thought of cruelty, wickedness, hatred, deceit or sensuality. Every thought, therefore, every idea (although the words, 'idea' and 'thought' mean two different things) has its own form, colour and dimension. This is why the Initiates see and envisage the world as a creation, a condensation of thought, of divine thought.

I have already explained to you that when a man has divine thoughts and desires they assume immediate reality somewhere in the universe, and also in the man himself. And when men are evil, vindictive and cruel, their thoughts and desires also become a reality, in some form or another, somewhere in the world, as well as in themselves. This cannot be seen at once, of course, but, sooner or later, everything will be seen. Another thing you must know is that poisonous plants and ferocious animals are fed, sustained and nourished by the evil thoughts and feelings of human beings. Yes, the venom distilled by human beings goes to reinforce the malignity of these animals and plants. Whereas the good thoughts and feelings of all visible and invisible creatures go to reinforce all that gives beauty, charm and fragrance to nature. Without knowing it, therefore, we participate in both the best and the worst of creation.

The thing that prevents human beings from understanding the effects of their thoughts and feelings is the fact that these effects are not immediately apparent. But you should not need immediate effects in order to be convinced. People say, 'We can't see any of that; it is impossible to believe it!' Initiates, on the other hand, have taken the time and trouble to observe, examine and verify what happens in nature, and they know that everything ends by coagulating, condensing. The crystallization of salts is an illustration of what happens throughout nature. You look at a liquid solution in which a chemist has dissolved some salts. 'The liquid is perfectly clear', you say; 'It's pure water.' But the chemist says, 'Wait; lets heat it.' and, under the influence of heat, the crystals begin to form. If you give salts the proper conditions they will crystallize. And man has a great many things in his head: you only have to give them the right conditions and you will see them crystallizing, materializing in acts.

But now I must tell you that thought can also be materialized in another way. Suppose somebody wants to put some salt in his soup by the power of thought alone: well, as I have already said, it is much better to use your hand to put salt in your soup! But if someone knows the laws of materialization of thought as they are practised in spiritualistic seances, he will be able to materialize a fluidic hand and, with that hand, which is condensed but still invisible, he will pick up the salt and sprinkle it into his soup. Thought, therefore, is capable of touching matter, but to do so it needs the intermediary of another plane; it has to be enveloped in etheric matter, which is denser than thought, and this etheric matter makes direct contact with physical matter, for they both belong to the same region and have much in common. You must understand, though, that Initiates are not at all interested in producing phenomena of this kind. Not because they are incapable of doing so, but because activities of this kind are uneconomical; why waste so much time and energy in order to put salt in your soup when it is so easy to use your hand?

'But then', you will ask; 'what do Initiates concentrate on?' They spend their time working to produce beneficial transformations in men's heads. For, once transformations take place in men's heads, their heads will find ways of communicating with their hearts and their hearts with their wills and, in this way, human beings will, eventually, move in the right direction. Isn't this a much more useful activity than to concentrate on moving, lifting or bending heavy objects? For when you spend your time and energy on activities of that kind, you are not doing anything in the hearts, souls or minds of men in order to improve and instruct them and bring them closer to God. Some yogis and magicians concentrate on trivial,

How Thought is Materialized on the Physical Plane

unimportant phenomena of this kind, whereas true Sages will say: 'All that is possible, to be sure. We can do it, too, but what would be the point? We would only be wasting a lot of time and energy and what would we gain? So little! No, it is simply not worth it. We prefer to spend all our energy on another kind of work which is millions of times more important for the future of mankind.' Yes, that is the reasoning of the wise. And I advise you to imitate them. The knowledge we possess must be used exclusively for a work that is really worthwhile and very important for the future of mankind.

So, what are we doing here, in the Universal White Brotherhood? We are working to build bridges. Yes, I have said it before: you are all bridge-builders; you are building bridges between yourselves and the sun, between your thought and matter and, as bridge-building is a delicate and complicated business, it takes a very long time. But once the whole system is in place, you will see how beautifully everything works! You will only have to push one button and the whole factory will start to hum as the machines begin to function... on condition, of course, that all the wiring and connections are properly installed.

Look at a watch, for example: it has a spring that sets in motion a complex system of wheels and gears in which each one transmits movement to the next one and, eventually, to the hands which tell you what time it is. The spring is not directly connected to the hands; the movement would be too sudden and uncontrollable; there have to be intermediaries between them to control and regulate their movement. This is the only way to get the hands to keep time, for one of them is very slow on the uptake, the other is a little more rapid and the third counts the seconds for runners, so it goes as fast as it can! So, here again, you see, there are intermediaries between the principle which gives the initial impetus and the organs which carry out a command or indicate a result. And there are a lot of other mechanisms in a watch which can also be seen in the human body. Anyone who knows how to observe and reason properly will recognize this great truth in the fields of physics, chemistry, biology, geography, history, sociology and psychology... absolutely everywhere.

If the physical body or the earth is to be transformed, there must, first of all, be contact, communication with the world of the spirit, with Heaven, or, if you prefer, with Plato's world of Ideas, that is to say, with the intelligible world, the world of archetypes. And, for me, this is nothing less than the divine world. These channels of communication pass through the soul: the spirit can only reach the domain of matter through the intermediary of the soul and, on the level of the human body, these correspond to the nervous and circulatory systems. The nervous system is closer to the domain of the spirit, and the circulatory system is closer to matter. The nervous system is analogous to the air which feeds fire, that is to say: the spirit; the circulatory system is analogous to the water that nourishes the earth, that is to say: the physical body. You must study these two intermediaries, air and water, which find their correspondence, on the physical plane, in thought and feeling. An Idea, on the other hand, exists on a much higher level. An Idea is linked to fire, to the spirit, the sun; and it is the world of Ideas that influences the world of thoughts. A thought is already more material than an Idea and it is always closely associated with feelings. If you think, for example, that someone you love is becoming really harmful and dangerous to you, observe your reactions: your feelings towards him will begin to change, you will no longer be so fond of him. What causes your feelings to change? The thoughts you entertain. On the other hand, if you discover that the friendship of someone for whom you have never felt any special affection could be very beneficial, that it is Providence that has brought you together for your own good, you will begin to love him.

One's feelings vary, therefore, according to one's thoughts; I am sure you have all experienced this time and again. And once your feelings are involved, they urge you to act, for feelings always need to express themselves in acts. You are thinking of a woman: if you have no special feeling for her, you will perhaps think that she is pretty, perhaps even very beautiful, but that is all: you will leave her alone. But then your feelings get involved and, immediately, you begin to take the initiative! Feelings don't waste time, they set your body in motion at once, and off you go to buy flowers for her, to court her, to kiss her! Before your feelings were involved, even though you recognized that she was charming and truly lovely, your reaction was: 'There's nothing to get excited about!' But once your feelings are involved, the situation changes, for they are closely related to matter and express themselves materially by setting in motion a chain of reactions.

Don't try to touch matter directly by means of thought; you won't succeed. Thought is principally designed to guide us, to enable us to know and to understand; it cannot affect matter unless the heart is also involved. As long as feeling and desire have not been aroused you will do nothing. Oh, of course, you may sometimes do things that are dictated by reason, but you will do them without conviction or pleasure. Some people never feel anything and they still act. Yes, but they act like automatons. Whereas, when feelings are involved, it is a very different matter! This does not necessarily mean that actions inspired by feelings are any better. Often, in fact, they are worse, for people sometimes do things without understanding why; all they know is that their feelings are urging them to act and they hurry to obey the urge.

There is still a great deal more that could be said, but it would take too long and what I have just explained might not be quite so clear. The main thing to remember is that thought is a power, but that this power has to be properly understood. As long as you have not prepared the tool, the intermediary, the lever, the arm, it is no good believing that your thoughts will materialize on the physical plane; they will continue to float in the rarer atmosphere of the mental plane. They will be recorded, to be sure, but they will not produce any material results. Whereas, if you bring them down onto the plane of feeling, they will always produce results.

And now, let's look at the question of hypnotism. You give someone who is under hypnosis a piece of paper, saying, 'It's a rose. Smell it and tell me what you smell.' And the person will talk to you about the exquisite perfume of that rose. This is because he is in a hypnotic state in which thought materializes instantly, not on the physical plane, but on the mental plane. The subject has picked up your thought, because your thought and the words that accompanied it have actually formed a rose on the mental plane and, as he is no longer functioning on the physical plane, his sense of smell is subtler and can pick up a perfume that exists only on the mental plane. He really and truly smells the rose, therefore; he is not mistaken. Or again, you can give him a glass of water and tell him to drink it, saying, 'Here's a glass of brandy. It's going to make you drunk', and, sure enough, he drinks it and it really does make him drunk. What has happened? In this case, again, he is functioning on another plane and, on that plane, the water really is brandy. This proves that the power of thought is absolute and immediate, but on the mental plane.

Knowing this, you can build anything, accomplish anything, in a flash, but in the higher regions, not on the level of matter. Do you want mansions, parks, gardens, cars, dancing girls, singing birds? Whatever you want you can have, immediately. If you were a little more clairvoyant you would actually see them, for they are already a reality. You will object, 'But there's nothing there; I can't touch anything!' Ah, if you want to touch them, of course, it may well take several hundred more years! This is how you must understand the question.

You can do all kinds of experiments in this area. Suppose, for example, that there is a vicious wind blowing. You can say a few loving words to it to persuade it to be less harsh: 'How sweet and gentle you are! You're not wicked, on the contrary: you give me great pleasure!' and, after a few minutes... Oh, to be sure, it is not the wind that changes, it is you. Something in you changes, and the buffeting of the wind seems to you like the caresses of a lover! You have to know how to pronounce the right words and do a little auto-suggestion, but people forget to pronounce the necessary words and they think that auto-suggestion is lies and illusion. No, no; your suggestions are creations, subtle creations; you pick up something with your subtle antennae and your antennae transmit it to your skin or your taste-buds, that is to say to the sensitive cells of your physical body. A great many people can be influenced by suggestion in this way, even perfectly normal people. You would be astounded to learn how often people are influenced by suggestion! Yes, whole crowds. A man with a strong, clearly defined thought and a very powerful brain can say that something is thus and so and, immediately, everyone begins to feel the same thing. History is full of cases of this kind!

And now you must draw some conclusions: work with thought, but don't expect your thought to be realized immediately on the physical plane. You will say, 'Sometimes it is; sometimes I only have to say a few words to change my frame of mind completely.' That is true but, as I have just explained, the change has not occurred on the level of matter and crystallized forms, but on the astral and mental levels, and you have picked it up on those levels. This does not contradict what I have just said: the change may be immediate, but on a higher level. And if you yourself are on that higher level then, of course, your thought is immediately effective. As a matter of fact, thought can be materialized immediately on the physical level also. Some magicians are capable of producing or calming a storm, of causing or healing a disease, but this is because they have already worked to build the 'roads and bridges'. I certainly don't advise any of you to start trying to exert your power of thought to produce phenomena of this kind. Work with thought, yes, but on a higher level, by asking for all that is most beneficial for your own evolution and that of the whole world. If you do that you may be sure of results... And then arm yourselves with patience and be ready to wait!

My faith and trust are not based on a vacuum, on illusions, but on Science. Everything I believe, everything I hope for, everything I do, is founded on knowledge, and you too can enter, in all tranquillity, into this knowledge. If you don't get the results you hoped for, don't say that it is because all that you have learned is false; check your own equipment to see if there is not something missing somewhere along the line. Your car won't go if something is missing from the engine; your watch won't keep time if its works are full of dust. So, if something is not working as it should in your machinery, it is not the fault of the Science; it is because your own grasp of it is incomplete. As I have said: it is not astrology that makes mistakes, it is astrologers!

Why did we meditate for longer than usual today? Because the conditions were excellent. Good conditions can come from the outside world or from yourselves. Sometimes you are more united with each other; your desire to create a climate of understanding, harmony and unity is stronger. When the right conditions exist, something marvellous takes shape within the Brotherhood; then our possibilities for creation are unlimited.

Yes, for the creations of the spirit are true creations. You cannot see them? That doesn't matter: don't bother about the question of whether you can see them or not. The only thing that matters is that they are real. And by your faith in them, you will be hastening their incarnation in the world of matter and facilitating the work of all the luminous spirits in the world, this work in which, one day, you are all destined to participate fully and consciously. You will ask, 'If this is our work, why don't we manage to do it?' Because you are not ready: the intermediaries are not in place, you have not developed them properly yet.

How Thought is Materialized on the Physical Plane

Until now, you did not even know about them, and how can one work with something one knows nothing about? But now that you are aware that these intermediaries exist, and you know how important they are, you will be able to develop and perfect them, and then, all together, we shall be capable of fantastic creations.

A certain number of you have already begun to create, but your creations are still unstable, weedy little hybrids, because their 'fathers and mothers' were not really very convinced or very conscious of what they were doing; their thoughts wandered in all directions. It all depends on the parents, whether they have beautiful, strong, vigorous children or not. There are days when you are more aware, more attuned to your divine ideal and more determined to work to attain it. But there are other days when you think, 'Well, I'll just give myself a little treat today. Tomorrow I'll get back onto the straight and narrow...' Do as you please, but don't be surprised if your thought produces no effect.

There is still a great deal to be said about antennae, also. Our antennae are designed to pick up waves and vibrations, and transmit them to other instruments; everybody knows that. But the question is to learn how to use our spiritual antennae to steer ourselves in the right direction. By contrast with the physical antennae of radios and televisions which remain fixed in one place, our spiritual antennae are mobile, extremely mobile in fact, because they are alive. They are like a series of tuning forks in which each branch, depending on its length, vibrates in response to the wavelengths to which it is tuned, with which it has an affinity. You can illustrate this with an experiment of your own: arrange a series of tuning forks of different lengths in such a way that they can vibrate, and then play different notes on the piano. For each note you play, the fork that is in perfect affinity with the wave that strikes it will vibrate in response. It is a medium. In fact, this is what human mediums are: tuning forks which pick up different wavelengths.

And man, too, is a tuning fork. If he wants to pick up waves from Heaven he has to shorten the branches of his antennae; the longer they are, the more he will receive waves from Hell. Man has the power to lengthen or shorten his antennae because they are alive, and it depends on him to make contact and vibrate to the wavelengths he chooses and to which he adjusts his antennae. Of course, when I speak of lengthening or shortening your antennae, it is a manner of speaking; you can use any other image you like to express the idea that man can be more spiritual or more materialistic. The more materialistic a man is, the more he receives communications from the lower regions; the subtler and more spiritual he is, the more intense his life becomes and the more closely he is tuned to the wavelength of Heaven. It all depends on him, for he possesses every possibility within himself.

Here, then, is an immense field of work, open to all those who want to become true creators. If you are highly evolved, you will orientate your antennae to pick up the messages of heavenly entities. But, if you are not very highly evolved, you will inevitably pick up transmissions from the inhabitants of the lower worlds. Unfortunately, this is what often happens: those who are not interested in advancing and becoming perfect, receive a continuous stream of communication from the very lowest regions; this is why they suffer from obsessions and hallucinations and are incapable of getting rid of them. Clinics and hospitals are filled with people who are a prey to all kinds of delusions. There is only one way to cure oneself, and that is to rise to a higher level.

The higher you rise into the upper regions, the more the inhabitants are intelligent, harmonious, luminous and full of love. Every contact you manage to have with the Angels, Archangels and Divinities of these regions is always a blessing, because they bring you their light and love. There are days when you are bursting with happiness; everything in you seems to sing; you have the impression that you understand everything.

And then, on other days, it is just the opposite: you feel utterly wretched, as though you were disintegrating... Yes, because you have been tuned to a different region and the message you picked up was not the same. I am not talking about the cause of this. I am well aware that there are many different circumstances that could be responsible for putting you into such a state: you have just had some bad news; someone has wronged you, etc. But that is not what I am talking about at the moment: I am only concerned with the type of communication you have had, and I say that you have been in touch with entities who were less intelligent and less kind and loving. When you venture into swampy regions infested by mosquitoes, or into forests where wild beasts and reptiles roam, you are, obviously, going to suffer; the mere presence of these animals is enough to cause you distress. But as soon as you reach other regions, and find yourself amongst hospitable, sympathetic beings who welcome you and offer you food and drink, it is wonderful! So, you must avoid putting yourself in contact with the lower regions and ensure that you are always in contact with Heaven.

In conclusion, let me come back, once again, to this question of thought. Do not attempt to influence matter by your thought: you won't succeed. Thought can only act on matter if the heart gets involved and urges the will to action. Remember, above all, that the mechanism of the psychic life is admirably expressed in the image of the sun which can only model the earth through the intermediary of air and water. If you fully understand this process, you will be capable of wonderful achievements. The entire science of white magic and theurgy is contained in this image of the four elements: sun, air, water and earth.

Sèvres, 13 May 1962

Chapter Seven

MEDITATION

Those of you who are here for the first time are, perhaps, astonished to see how often we pause for a long moment of silence. You don't understand why we do that, so you think, 'I'm wasting my time here! If I'd stayed at home I could have been doing masses of things. What are all these weird people doing? I've never seen such faces... What have I got myself into? I think I'd better go away again at once!' Yes, this is quite an interesting and entertaining question! So, although I have already talked to you about meditation very often, I want to talk to you about it again today.

Some of you will probably say that you have read books about meditation and have been meditating for years, now, so you know what it is! Yes, there are any number of books about meditation, these days, particularly books by Hindus. In fact, I am sure that everybody meditates at some time or another. Oh, yes, wonderful meditations! When you are tired and sleepy, you meditate and your head nods in time to your meditation to show that it approves! Yes... a profound meditation! Cynics might say that you are dozing, but let's just say that you begin by meditating and end by dozing!

But, let's be serious and look at the question of meditation from a philosophical point of view. People often use the word 'meditate' without any real understanding of what it means. Man has never understood what an extraordinarily powerful instrument it can be; how much it can contribute to his full development, and also what great changes and transformations it can operate, not only in his own, personal life, but in the life of his family, of society and of the entire world. Above all, men do not know how to prepare the conditions that thought needs in order to manifest itself freely.

Generally speaking, meditation is not a habit that most human beings have cultivated to any great extent. From time to time, when a difficulty arises, when someone is faced with a particularly knotty problem or a very painful situation, he will become pensive and more thoughtful because he has to find a way out of his problems. But this cannot really be qualified as meditation; it is simply an instinctive, natural response to danger or disaster. When a man finds himself in danger he instinctively reaches for help by turning his gaze inwards; he even begins to pray, to ask for help from the Being that he neglected when things were going well for him. He remembers that when he was a child his parents told him that this Supreme Being was all-powerful, omniscient and all-loving, so now that he has problems, he instinctively turns back to Him and, with the utmost humility in the presence of such extraordinary power, asks Him for help. Yes, but the thing is that this only happens in extreme circumstances: in moments of danger, war, illness or death.

In the ordinary way, when people are perfectly happy and content, they have no desire to pray or meditate; they don't think it is necessary; they don't see the use of it. When everything is going well, people see no reason to wander off into the vague, nebulous world of meditation. But when things go wrong, when they are unhappy or in great difficulty, and they realize that concrete, material solutions are inadequate, then they turn inwards and look for help and solutions to their problems in the world above.

Meditation

From time immemorial, Initiates have always told us that man possessed a very powerful tool: the tool of thought, and that if he knew how to work with it, he could obtain tremendous results. Obviously, if someone fails to obtain results; if he feels neither freer nor more at peace nor more enlightened, he will see no point in continuing the effort. Many people try to meditate, once, twice, three times... even ten times, and when they don't succeed they decide to abandon such a useless exercise! But you must realize that, if you fail to get any results, it is because you don't really know what true meditation is. Meditation is, first and foremost, an activity of thought in which you concentrate on an idea or an image in order to study and understand it and see how it ties in with other ideas and images and where it stands in relation to the whole. You can take almost anything as a subject of meditation: beauty, strength, the will, space, immortality, the Deity... the possibilities are endless. The only essential condition, without which there can be no meditation, is that no outside care or preoccupation must be allowed to interfere with the work of your thought.

When someone begins to meditate, he is on the threshold between two worlds: a world above, Heaven, and a world below, Hell. He is in an intermediary zone in which he has the power to set in motion elements, forces and entities either of light or of darkness. A man who meditates, therefore, can use his power of thought either to construct or to destroy, to create order or to disrupt it and, naturally, if he is not enlightened and intelligent, he will disturb more than he arranges. Physically, chemically and mechanically, whether he knows it or not, he begins to set in motion forces and elements for good or for evil, for construction or for destruction.

Thought is a tremendously powerful instrument given to us by Nature; you must be aware of this and realize that, by means of this instrument, you can make contact with certain regions and set certain forces in motion, and that this is of paramount importance for good or evil, for health or sickness. You must have a deep sense of the importance of thought as a potent magical process. Most people are unconscious of what they stir up with their thought, and then, when calamity strikes, they are surprised! Well, instead of being surprised, they should realize that meditation is a process by which formidable forces are set in motion in the subconscious and the superconscious, in one's whole being and in the whole of nature.

A lot of people close their eyes and imagine that they are meditating, but their thought... Where is their thought? Everywhere and nowhere, wandering aimlessly in every direction; is there any wonder that this kind of 'meditation' benefits no one? Initiates, Sages and great Masters have always envisaged meditation as the most potent means available to man, without which he can never achieve anything really solid and constructive. Without meditation you cannot arrive at self-knowledge or self-dominance, you cannot develop qualities and virtues. It is precisely because human beings have not given meditation a position of pre-eminence that their spiritual life, their inner drive and aspirations are always so feeble.

People have sometimes said to me: 'I've been trying to meditate for years, but my brain always seems to get stuck and I never get anywhere.' I have already given several lectures at the Bonfin about this, and explained that, in order to meditate, you must prepare yourself in advance; if your life is littered with all kinds of obstacles that you have neglected to tidy up, they will get in the way of your meditation. Suppose you come up to the Rock in the morning and settle down to meditate, thinking: 'Ah, now I'm going to meditate; I'm going to contemplate the sun and link up with those inexhaustible forces and energies that the Master talks about, etc...' and suppose that, in spite of your excellent intentions, you simply cannot manage to concentrate, and that this pattern repeats itself day after day: after a time you will simply abandon the effort.

Meditation

Why do you so often fail in your attempts to concentrate? Because you have never understood that the different moments of your life are not separate units. Each moment is connected to all those that have gone before and which we lump together and call 'the past'. It is this past that gets in your way and, as you are sincerely anxious to meditate, you do violence to your brain and it seizes up and refuses to function. Yes, simply because it never occurred to you, the day before, to get your brain and your whole being ready in order to attend the sunrise the next morning; it never occurred to you to cleanse yourself and put everything in order so as to be capable of doing some work with the rising sun. Suppose you have been quarrelling with someone: the next morning, when you are trying to meditate, the past comes back to you and you go over the quarrel in your mind, remembering all the insults you gave and received, and planning what to say to him when you meet again. So much for your meditation! It has turned into a mental free-for-all! Instead of rising to divine regions, you will have spent your time going over and over the past, unable to shut out the endless stream of people and events that comes crowding into your mind. And the same thing repeats itself year after year: no wonder your meditations don't get results!

Man is capable of becoming all-powerful, but only if he knows a certain number of truths and, in particular, the truth that every moment of our lives is connected to all those that have gone before. Someone who reasons correctly will think: 'First of all I'm not going to eat too much so as not to overload my digestive system. Also, I'm not going to go and discuss things with so-and-so, because goodness only knows what that would lead to, and I'd be incapable of meditating tomorrow!' A disciple, therefore, prepares himself in advance by purifying himself, by refusing to overload himself with useless preoccupations, by getting enough sleep. And, above all, he develops to the highest possible degree his desire to improve and perfect himself in order to help others and be an example, a model, a true son of God. In accordance with Jesus' instructions to his disciples, he is animated by the sublime desire to do the will of God in everything. But wishing and wanting alone will not enable us to carry out the precepts Jesus gave us: there are also a certain number of things that we need to know. A great many people want to live according to these precepts, but they fail because they do not know how to set about it. If you have left the hot-water tap running or the gas turned on, or forgotten the baby in the bath, it will come back to you in a flash just as you are about to meditate... and that will be the end of your meditation!

Prepare yourself in advance, therefore, and when you are free in body, mind and feelings, when you have finally escaped from the prison of your everyday life, you will become sensitive to purity, limpidity and peace, to the sun. And then you will sing your gratitude to Heaven as you rise within yourself and begin to perceive that there is another life, a life that is so new, vast, broad and deep that you feel yourself expanding in it and drawn out of yourself into another, higher region. And this higher region, in reality, is within you. Yes, this divine life flows within you, and in experiencing it, you experience a few moments of true Life. Illuminated by this dazzling perception, you will exclaim, 'Dear God, at last I have actually seen that a world of sublime beauty really does exist. Why, oh why, have I spent my whole life immersed in impurity and disorder?' In this way the divine world begins to awaken within you, and once this has happened, you can never forget it; henceforth you have the conviction that the soul is a reality, that the divine world exists and that countless creatures inhabit it. Why this firm conviction? Because you have succeeded in setting in motion forces that were previously unknown to you, forces far more powerful and beneficial than any you had ever known, for, before this, you were in the grip of other, hostile, corrosive forces which were gradually destroying you.

This is something that has always been known and taught by Initiates. Meditation is a psychological and philosophical question; it is also an act of cosmic dimensions of the greatest importance. Once a disciple has tasted the sweetness of this higher world his convictions are strengthened and he can feel that his faculties begin to obey him. When he wants to set his mind to work it obeys him, and when he wants it to stop it stops; it is as though the cells of his whole being had decided to conform to his desires. As long as he has not reached this mastery, it takes him hours and days to find inner peace, because his cells continue their restless movement and refuse to listen to him. They say: 'If you think you can scare us you're making a big mistake! We can't take you seriously and we're certainly not afraid of you. We have no respect for you because you have shown how stupid and ignorant you are!' and they go on doing exactly as they please. You all know what I am talking about, don't you? And then, on other days, you find that your cells obey you because, knowingly or unknowingly, you have reached a higher level and released higher forces and, in doing so, have gained greater command over your cells, for they recognize a hierarchical authority and are ready to obey their lord and master.

After all, isn't this true in every area of life? In businesses and government or in the armed forces, every individual strives to move up the hierarchical ladder and become manager, chairman of the board, chief of staff or general, because when he reaches the top and, especially, when he sports all his ribbons and medals, others respect and obey him. Even if a man is a complete idiot or a tyrant, it makes no difference: it is his rank that commands obedience. And where do you suppose that this sense of hierarchy comes from? It is not a human invention, for human beings invent nothing. Through intuition, instinct or trial and error, they simply discover what already exists in nature, and hierarchy is something that exists throughout nature. In the heavens (stars and constellations), on earth (rivers, mountains, trees and animals) and even in man, everything is ordered hierarchically.

And since this is so, since it is common knowledge that someone who wants to be a leader and impose his will on others has to be at least one step above them, why should it be difficult to understand that in spiritual things too, we have to be a step above our own inhabitants if we want them to obey us? The principle and the practical applications are the same on all levels. And this is precisely the aim of an Initiate: to win the obedience of his own inner world. He is not interested in being obeyed by mountains, stars, animals or men; he is only interested in achieving self-dominance, in being the master of his own physical body, of his own thoughts and feelings, and he works constantly to this end.

Spiritual exercises such as meditation, concentration, contemplation and prayer, enable man to free himself progressively from this prison, these chains that hold him in bondage to the subterranean world. So many have been caught and held captive! Lacking the light, they let themselves sink lower and lower, deep into this fearful world. Call it Hell, call it the Devil, it makes no difference; it is a very real world in which many are inextricably lost, simply because they did not choose to use the means of salvation taught by Initiatic Science. They thought they were being very intelligent whereas, in fact, they were simply being stubborn and proud... and look where they are now!

The only way to escape from torment and anguish is to meditate. But, as I have already said, in order to meditate one first has to settle a certain number of questions. When the mother of a large family wants to make a cake, for instance, she waits until the children are in bed and asleep before she begins; she cannot get anything done while they are all round her, clinging to her skirts and clamouring for attention. And we have to do the same: we have this large family within us, all those noisy, high-spirited children, and we must make them keep quiet so as to be free to do our work, and then, once it is done, we can go back to them and share out the cake!

If you understand that meditation is the key to your salvation, that it is the most effective means to do a tremendous work of inner transformation, you will obtain results. But don't try to do it without taking into account all the other elements, otherwise there will always be some loose ends, things that don't quite fit and that distract and pester you during your meditation. This is what Jesus meant when he said that we should not worry about the morrow. Yes, because if you live as you should today, the morrow will find you free: you will be in a position to dispose of yourself at will and concentrate your thoughts on the subject of your choice, because yesterday's affairs will all be in order. Whereas, if your life is full of loose ends, you will find yourself handicapped by them and have to race about in all directions trying to set things straight and remedy your past mistakes; you will not be free either to work in the present or to create the future.

Some of you may say: 'As far as I'm concerned, I don't know what meditation is and I don't want to know. I'm willing to make sacrifices; I'm ready to be charitable and do good to others, and that's enough!' No, that is not enough, for our actions can transgress certain laws, complicate things and even be very destructive if we do not begin by meditating. Why? Because only meditation clears our vision and allows us to see reality as it is.

You can meditate on all kinds of subjects: health, beauty, wealth, intelligence, power, glory, the Angels, the Archangels and the Heavenly Hierarchies. All of these subjects are good, but the best of all is to meditate on God Himself in order to be steeped in His love, light and strength, in order to live for a brief moment in His eternity... and always to meditate in order to serve God, to do His will and be one with Him. No meditation is more beneficial or more powerful than this. Any other kind of meditation is motivated by some form of self-interest: hopes of financial advantage, the will to use occult forces for personal enrichment or to gain power over others. Initiates understand that what is most advantageous for them is, precisely, not to seek their own personal advantage, but to seek to become servants of God. All the rest has a slight odour of black magic or witchcraft to it. Yes, without realizing it, most occultists dabble in witchcraft. They use these invisible forces to gain wealth and power or to enthral women, not for the service of God. So, you see, there are many different shades and degrees of meditation!

Obviously, one has to begin by meditating on something accessible. Human beings are so designed that it is not natural to them to exist in an abstract environment. They need to hold on to something visible and tangible, something close to them and that they love. It is very easy, for instance, to concentrate on food when one has not eaten for a long time. It takes no special effort to be like that cat we were talking about, which concentrated so hard on the mouse! We don't need to try: it just happens, all by itself. And think of how a young man concentrates on the girl he loves: for hours and even days on end, simply because he loves her. And here, too, there is no need for any special effort, but what a meditation! He can't tear himself away!

So, begin by meditating on something that gives you pleasure, something you enjoy. Later, you can go on to other things, but begin with something you really like, something that attracts you (of course it must be something spiritual, not just anything). In this way, by beginning with subjects that are already congenial to you, you will develop your own means and methods of work and, later on, you can leave these subjects and move on to greater heights, to more distant, more abstract regions. It is obvious that if you begin by trying to meditate on space, time and eternity, you will not get very far! Later on, you will be capable of fixing your thoughts on such things as the void, the depths of nothingness and so on, but begin with something easier and then, gradually, you can move on to more abstract subjects.

However, I must repeat what I said earlier: the most sublime meditation is to be in communion with God, to submit to Him, to want to serve Him and be nothing more than an instrument in His hands. When you melt into the Lord in this way, all the divine qualities, all His power, love and wisdom, all His immensity floods into you and, one day, you will become a divinity. When they hear this, some people object: 'What pride to think that you can become a divinity!' But let them read the Gospels. Didn't Jesus say 'Be ye perfect as your heavenly Father is perfect'? There is no ideal higher than this and it was Jesus himself who gave it to us, but Christians have forgotten that. A great many of them think that it is sufficient to go and light a candle in church from time to time and, for the rest, to look after one's own little chicken-run in order to be good Christians. What an exalted ideal! As though the Kingdom of God would ever be any nearer if everybody behaved like that! Oh, those poor Christians; they hold strictly to the principle that one must not ask too much of human beings for fear of falling into the sin of pride! Well, what I am telling you is exactly the opposite: we must harbour the highest possible ideal in our hearts, souls and spirits and let the ignorant say what they like!

Human beings need to be instructed; they need to learn the right methods, and one of these methods is meditation. What can you do with meditation? Everything! Once your thought has been set free, you can explore all the regions of the universe and meet all the creatures that dwell in it. You think of light, for example, and instantly, there you are, floating, swimming in light, submerged in a flood of colour. You wish to make contact with perfumes or music: immediately you can smell sweet perfumes and hear symphonies. You want to know what life is like up there, in Heaven: you concentrate, make contact with heavenly beings and ask them, and they reveal their life to you.

By means of meditation one enters into a world more real than reality. But when one is too deeply immersed in one's own worries and preoccupations, one has no time to explore this other world. This is why most Westerners neglect meditation. They consider it a waste of time. Of course, it goes without saying that if someone does not respect the preliminary conditions, if he does not prepare himself in advance, he will not get any results from his meditation and, in that case, it *will* be a waste of time. Yes, but that is because it was not practised in the proper conditions. And this is how people draw false conclusions. All Initiates and mystics who have prepared the necessary conditions, have experienced such overwhelming revelations and such sublime ecstasy, that all the wealth and glory of the earth fade to nothing in comparison with the sensations of fulfilment and immensity, with the light obtained from their meditations; they ask for nothing more. Yes, my dear brothers and sisters, it is so beautiful, so marvellous, that once one has experienced these sublime states one begins to be less and less preoccupied by worldly things. To be sure, one must keep a sense of proportion here, too. I am not saying that you should give up everything else in favour of meditation. That would be exaggerated and I hold no brief for exaggeration. I am only saying that you must give first place, attach much more importance to your spiritual life. Is that clear?

And now, let me tell you the two best subjects of meditation. I have already talked a little about the first, which is to become a totally compliant instrument in the hands of God, so that God Himself may think, feel and act through you. You abandon yourself to the will of Wisdom and Light and put yourself totally at the service of omniscient Light so that the Light, which possesses all knowledge, may guide you in all your ways.

But man is also on earth and what is he on earth for? In the Lord's Prayer, Jesus said (you see, I always refer to what Jesus said, for he said it all! What would be the point of inventing anything else?). So, Jesus said: 'Thy will be done on earth as it is in Heaven'. 'On earth as in Heaven' means that the earth must be a mirror of Heaven. And the 'earth' is our own, personal earth, the earth of our physical body. So this means that once we have worked to reach the summit, the spirit, we must descend to work at the organization of our physical body. Immortality is on high, light is on high, harmony, peace, beauty and all subtle realities are on high. And everything that exists on high must be brought down and become incarnate here below, on the physical level.

Ask to become a servant of God, therefore, and, at the same time, work at the formation of that other body within you that we call the Body of Light, the Body of Glory, the Immortal Body, the Body of Christ. The Gospels speak of this body, too, but Christians have never paid much attention to it. The truth of the matter is that they are not really interested in understanding the Gospels in depth: they are anything but real Christians! You may feel that to tend the earth is not a very glorious ideal, whereas Hindus... Yes, I know: Hindus and Buddhists are only interested in escaping from this earth of sorrow, suffering and strife and reaching Nirvana. I know; that is their philosophy, but it is not the philosophy of Christ. Christ's philosophy is to bring Heaven down to earth, to bring about the Kingdom of God and His Righteousness on earth. This is the Kingdom that Jesus was working for, and he asked his disciples to work for it also. So that is what we have to do: work for the coming of the Kingdom of God on earth and, to begin with, in our own physical bodies. This is the true philosophy. I am not interested in what others may have understood. I have devoted years to learning what Christ thought, and now I know.

'Thy will be done on earth as it is in Heaven.' Yes, but where are the labourers for this work? Men have other philosophies in their heads, and this means that they will have to keep coming back to earth until they manage to turn it into a Garden of Eden. When they have done this, they will go to another planet, leaving the earth to the animals, which also have to evolve. This surprises you, doesn't it? You have never heard anything like this from the pulpit! You see, men have been sent to earth to work as labourers on a building site, but they are not interested in their work; they are only interested in having a good time. You must not neglect your duty in that way: every day you must work to transform the earth into a Paradise. If you do this the Lord will commend you, saying: 'Well done. You have been good and faithful servants and worked well in my fields. Now it is time for you to enter into the Joy and Glory of My Kingdom.' In the Gospels, too, Jesus speaks of labourers who are sent out to work in the fields. Well, it is we who are those labourers. And where are the fields in which we are working? And what have we planted?

You are certainly familiar, also, with the parable of the talents. The idea is the same. The unprofitable servant who was punished because he had buried his talents represents all those who don't work, who are only interested in making money, having a good time and making the earth a more comfortable place for themselves. This has nothing to do with Christ's philosophy. We have been sent to earth with a specific task, and when we have done it, the Lord will give us all the rest; the whole universe will be ours. This is why it saddens me to see the conception that so many occultists and so-called spiritualists and mystics have of life on this earth. They marry and have children, eat, drink and make merry exactly like the most ignorant of men. What are they doing about the work for which they have been sent to earth? Exactly nothing! And this applies to you, too: take a close look into yourselves and you will see that what you do bears no relation to Christ's philosophy.

There! What I have given you today are the two best subjects for meditation: how to devote yourselves entirely to the service of the Godhead, and how to go about bringing the whole of Heaven down to earth as a concrete, physical reality. The meaning of life is contained in these two activities. All other activities have a certain significance, of course, but no other activity has this divine significance. God has created man in his own image; He has created man so that he shall come to resemble Him. And if you don't believe this, go and ask Him!

All my life I have searched for what is best, and I have found it. But to have found it is no reason to sit back and twiddle one's thumbs. Quite the contrary: now is the time to set to work, because that which has been 'found' must now be translated into concrete reality here, on earth, just as it already exists in Heaven. The fact that many things do already exist here, on earth, on the mental level, is not sufficient. They must also be made to exist on the physical level, and it is this that is long and difficult.

To be sure, there is a great deal more to be said about this, but that is enough for today. You must understand the importance of meditation and, above all, that if your meditations are to bear fruit, you must watch over your thoughts, feelings and actions, in other words, over your whole way of life. Begin by meditating on simple, easy subjects and, gradually, you can go on to more sublime things and, one day, all your work will be focused on becoming an instrument in the hands of God in order to bring Heaven down to earth. There is nothing more divine or more glorious than this. This is the perfect fulfilment of all divine laws, of all wisdom.

Lausanne, 23 May 1963

Chapter Eight

**THE HUMAN INTELLECT
AND COSMIC INTELLIGENCE**

The Master reads the Meditation for the day:
'It is not necessary to understand silence. Silence is something that has to be felt, for true understanding starts with feeling. The time is coming when we shall speak to each other and understand each other in silence.'

This is a very rich, very profound thought. I have already spoken to you several times about the heart and the intellect, and explained that man's heart, that is to say, his faculty of feeling, is much older than his intellect; the heart developed long before the intellectual faculties. This is why Initiates often speak of the 'intelligence of the heart'. To understand with one's heart is to feel, to experience. But human beings have gradually neglected this form of understanding in favour of an intellectual approach; they think that they have to read and study in order to understand. To be sure, the intellect has tremendous possibilities for exploration and comprehension, but its scope is restricted to the objective, material dimension; this is why it is true to say that true understanding is not within the power of the intellect.

I have already spoken to you several times about the two worlds, the objective and the subjective, and given you many arguments and examples showing that the intellect gave rise to science and philosophy, whereas the heart gave rise to religion and ethics. To give you a clearer understanding of these two aspects, take the example of a sphere described by two different observers; one of them is inside the sphere, and one outside, and they both have their opinion. Obviously, the observer on the outside of the sphere declares that it is convex, whilst the one on the inside declares that it is concave; and as both are convinced that they are right, the argument never ends! Science, which studies the external, objective world, has formed an opinion about the universe (the sphere represents the universe), and scientists write and explain and teach that opinion. And what they tell us is true, but it is true of only one side of the question, the external, objective side. Whereas he who finds himself on the inside of the sphere, in the domain of the heart and soul and spirit, has other notions, other ideas and another experience of life, of the universe and of everything in it. So who is right? Both; but neither is more than half right! A third person is needed to form a synthesis of the two points of view. The outside observer must be told, 'You are on the outside, and you are fifty per cent right in what you say.' And the inside observer must be told, 'You are on the inside, and you are fifty per cent right, too. But truth is one hundred per cent right, and it is I who possess the truth, because I can see things from both the inside and the outside. By means of my heart and soul I am on the inside, and by means of my intellect I am on the outside. I can see the whole reality, therefore, and I see that it has two aspects, two opposite and complementary manifestations'.

Religion is on the inside; it is the domain of the heart, of the soul, of mystical feeling. It can be felt and experienced, but it cannot be seen or touched; whereas the objective dimension studied by science, can be weighed and measured; it shows tangible results. And yet, it is the inner world that is the most important because, ultimately, it is what you experience within yourself that counts, not what is outside or alongside you. Reality is what you feel. If you feel that you are being persecuted, if you believe that you are being pursued by evildoers or monsters, even if they don't exist objectively, in the outside world, you can still be in an agony of terror because, for you, they are real. Similarly, you may possess great wealth, but if you have no inner perception of it, if you don't take advantage of it or rejoice in it, it is as though you had nothing. You see: we are obliged to conclude that it is the inner, subjective world, what you actually feel and experience, that is the most important. What we call objective reality is second in importance. In fact, objective reality is not true reality: reality is what you feel. If you feel the presence of Heaven, if you feel joy, splendour, wealth, freedom, strength or intelligence within yourself, does it really matter whether they exist or not on the outside? If you are in an inner state of joy and abundance, does it matter if your outer conditions are wretched? After all, experience is not an outer but an inner reality.

The priority belongs to the inner dimension, therefore. This is simple and obvious, and yet so many people fail to see it and continue to try to live in the external dimension. The trouble is that one cannot live in the external dimension: one can see it, observe and measure it, make drawings of it, but to live and experience it one is obliged to possess an inner dimension. If you have no sense of beauty, you can look at the most glorious manifestations of nature and feel nothing; if you have never developed your inner aesthetic sense you will remain cold and unmoved. Even the external, objective world cannot affect us if we are not inwardly awake. There are people who can remain totally indifferent at the spectacle of a sunrise or a beautiful lake, because they have never developed any sensitivity. Whereas an artist, for instance, only has to glimpse something to vibrate in response and start writing or composing, because a rich world of poetry is already alive within him.

To think that I have to try to convince human beings of such simple, elementary truths! But for them, the inner life simply does not exist. They are only interested in getting rich, in accumulating more and more money, in opening more and more branch offices, in swallowing up the whole world! In the meantime, they allow the inner faculties which would enable them to experience joy to atrophy. They have... they possess... and they are less and less capable of enjoying what they have. You see the same thing in men who sleep with every woman they meet and always want more, because they are never satisfied. They have never developed their inner sensitivity, and they think that, if they go on looking for love externally, they will eventually find it. But they never do. I have met countless men and women who spent their time in pursuit of the outward manifestations of love because they were incapable of any kind of inner feeling. They were inwardly paralysed!

Henceforth, instead of counting on externals, you must try to glimpse Heaven in the least little things. If you persistently look for external satisfactions, something inside inevitably withers and dies. If you eat substantial meals every day, several times a day, your appetite will lose its finer edge. It is this that most people fail to understand. Love in homoeopathic doses is marvellous, wonderful... but once you start taking it in allopathic doses, the sensations you enjoy will be less intense. To prove my point, look at a young man and girl who fall in love: to begin with, they live in a state of such poetic beauty that a rose petal that the boy receives from his sweetheart is enough to send him into raptures for hours on end; it becomes a talisman for him. But what is there in that petal? Nothing at all, perhaps. But, for him, it is redolent with the girls emanations, with her soul, her thought; he feels himself becoming a poet, a gallant knight, a hero for her sake. They don't even kiss each other, but the least little thing, a look, a touch of the hand, is enough to fill them with sweet memories for days and days, as though their souls contained the entire universe. But once they begin to take allopathic doses of love, the sensations they experience lose something of their subtlety; something within them fades and diminishes. So then, in the hope of intensifying their sensations, they begin to take bigger and bigger doses. It is the same process as in drug addiction: to begin with, a minute dose is wonderfully effective, but gradually, as the habit takes hold, it has less and less effect and the dose has to be increased until, in the end, the addict destroys himself.

It is because men do not know these laws that they do themselves so much harm. If they would only take homoeopathic doses of love they would find them far more effective because homoeopathic doses can be felt by their subtle bodies. The particles of our subtle bodies are not so tightly packed together as in our denser, material bodies, so they have more room to vibrate and dilate and rejoice, and their joy communicates itself to our whole being. The physical body cannot feel the effects of a homoeopathic dose; it reacts to strong, allopathic doses and then the vibrations of the spirit are weakened.

There are certain laws involved here. Homoeopathic doses do not have much effect on the physical body because the particles of the physical body are too compact, too tightly packed together; it takes a strong dose to affect them. But the etheric, astral and mental bodies are so subtle and tenuous that they can be affected by a minute homoeopathic dose. You will ask, 'But can't a homoeopathic dose affect the physical body?' Yes, it can; it reaches the physical body by way of the subtle bodies. A homoeopathic dose; a look, a word or a thought, for instance; affects your astral and mental bodies and it is their reactions which touch your physical body and produce beneficial or harmful effects. You don't need to hit someone or wound him physically in order to make his physical body ill or even kill him; a look full of hatred or a cruel word is enough. How does this happen? Through the intermediary of his astral and mental bodies. Your look or words can provoke sentiments of such horror and desolation in him that they affect even his physical body. On the other hand, if someone is ill in bed, you can say a few words of encouragement or touch him gently and he will immediately leap out of bed! What has happened? You have given him a homoeopathic dose. And who received that dose? His higher bodies; and the reactions of his higher bodies are reflected on the level of his physical body, where they restore certain currents and communications so that he instantly feels better.

Orthodox medicine will, perhaps, discover all these things one day. 'But' you will ask; 'why hasn't it discovered them already?' Because they are too obvious; it cannot see what is obvious! People are always looking for things that are far away; they never see what is in front of their faces. I see proof of this in the fact that I have been talking to you for thirty-four years about things that are under your noses but that you have never seen! Yes, that is my special talent: to keep showing you what is there, in front of you, day and night.

The intellect, which focuses all its attention on the external world, which observes, investigates and studies objective reality, possesses fifty percent of the truth. And yet, when I consider the relatively greater importance of the heart, of feelings, of what one actually experiences, I think I would give it more than fifty percent, because to live is far more important than to learn or to read a book. Of course, when you read and learn, you can know a great many things, but they remain superficial and theoretical, they don't touch the depths of your being. The things you read are recorded, to be sure, but only on a superficial level, so they can very quickly be wiped out: one day they simply leave you and you forget them. Look at all that you have already forgotten about the books you have read! And yet they were all recorded. Yes, but they were recorded on the surface, and what is on the surface is easily erased. And now compare that book learning with something that you have actually experienced, something that you have felt and tasted deep down: whatever else happens to you in life this is something that is impossible to forget! Why? Because it has

The Human Intellect and Cosmic Intelligence

been recorded at a much deeper level, at the very heart of your being.

Nine tenths of humanity spend their time on the surface of life; they are not alive, they feel nothing... Don't misunderstand me, when I say that they are not alive, I mean that they are incapable of experiencing an essential, sublime, divine reality. You have to live things and experience them on a deep level, only then will they stay with you for eternity. Yes, the only things you can take with you and which will never be wiped out, even when you die, are those that you have verified for yourself in your own life, your own soul, your own heart. All the rest, everything you have learned at the university or from books, will have to be left behind when you leave this world. You cannot take that knowledge with you because it is not really yours, it has never really become your own flesh and bone. It belongs to others, you took it from them or they lent it to you and, one day, it will leave you: you cannot take it with you. And when you come back to this world you will still not be free to dispose of it, you will have to go to school and read books and learn all over again: what a waste of energy!

As you can see, this means that human beings have to learn the same things over and over again. They cannot remember from one incarnation to the next, what they had learned, because they learned it in an intellectual, superficial, external, objective way. Whereas Initiates pick out the essence of reality and assimilate it in their lives. They discard all the rest, knowing that even if they do not do so consciously and deliberately they will be obliged to do so when the time comes for them to leave the earth. And you, too, must understand that if you assimilate what you know into your life, if you actually get the taste of it and verify it by putting it into practice so that it becomes your lifeblood, your very quintessence, then it will be truly yours: no one will ever be able to take it away from you. When you come back to earth you will bring your knowledge with you; you will not be obliged to learn it all over again from the beginning; you will go on adding true knowledge to that which you already have. Yes, this is how it is all organized.

But, how ignorant everybody is! Even scientists, philosophers and theologians are unaware of all these realities, and yet they are all so proud of their learning! But a few years hence, even they will have to admit that it has all vanished without a trace, all they have left is what they have verified, tasted, felt and experienced for themselves.

Now, I am not telling you not to read or study; on the contrary, you must do both. For look what happens when you come to this Initiatic School: you begin by studying. You cannot feel or taste or really experience the truths that I talk to you about, so you have to study them. The great difference here is that the emphasis is on life itself. And that changes everything. No one asks you to collect and store up all sorts of information so as to become a walking encyclopaedia! You are given some materials, of course, in other words you receive some instruction, but it is up to you to choose what suits you best, what is compatible with your particular temperament. You can leave the rest to one side, or give it to others! What matters is to build something essential with what you receive. Generally speaking, human beings do not use their knowledge to build anything useful. This is another weakness, a failing, that I detect in men of letters. They are journalists, authors, lecturers, etc., so, of course, they do something with it: they write novels or articles or they teach; but they do not construct their own house, their own temple, that is to say, their own future.

My task is to give you many different kinds of knowledge and information, but it is up to you to choose the materials you need, that is to say, a few methods from amongst all that, for some methods suit certain temperaments better than others. This is why I have often told you, 'I give you all kinds of information and different methods and points of view so that you can choose. I have to lay out all kinds of fruit and vegetables on the table and it is up to you to take whatever suits your taste and your capacity!' Just because there is a great variety of 'dishes' on the table, it does not mean that you have to eat everything and make yourselves sick! There were some brothers, in the past, who thought that they had to put every single thing I said into practice! No, no! You would kill yourself! For psychological and pedagogical reasons I have to give you something new every day, so that each one of you can find what is best for him or her. But you must choose just three or four exercises or methods. If you put them into practice all your life long you will get fantastic results from them, far more so than if you tried to apply thousands of different methods. That is what I did: I picked out a few truths, but I picked those that included all the others, that lay at the heart of reality; in this way, when I put them into practice I am in touch with the whole universe. I take care not to disperse my energies, because I know that when one spreads oneself too thin one accomplishes nothing.

You understand, now, why I always emphasize the importance of learning to feel things, to get the taste of them, and not only to get the taste of them, but to put them into practice. You must never be content to remain on the the surface, to see only the objective aspect of things. And, in this connection, I feel like saying something more.

Why has modern science strayed so far from the truth? Because it has chosen to study only the objective dimension. And yet there are many important truths in the subjective dimension. But these subjective truths are subtle, invisible and intangible, so they are ignored, in spite of the fact that they are more important than those of the objective dimension. Can you see your life? Can you touch it? No: then why do you attach so much importance to it? And your conscience: you can neither see it nor touch it, and yet a court of law demands that you tell the truth according to your conscience! And what about your thoughts and feelings? Yes, particularly your feelings: why do you continue to believe in the veracity of your feelings even in the face of contradictory evidence? Take the example of a young girl in love: you can use every imaginable argument to convince her that the boy she loves is no good, that he is a complete bounder, an absolute scoundrel... her only response will be: 'I love him!' That is all she wants to know. You can use any number of objective arguments and proofs, but she is only interested in her feelings, that is to say, in her subjective world. And what is so strange is that, in a different context, this same girl will deny the importance of the subjective dimension! As for scientists... I'd rather not even talk about their opinion: they simply despise the subjective aspect... until, of course, they are attacked by someone who says, 'Your money or your life!' Without hesitation then, every one of them will say, 'Take my money, but leave me my life!' Yes, but is their life visible? No; thoughts, feelings and life itself are invisible and yet, quite unconsciously, people give them priority.

Yes, instinctively, unconsciously, blindly, everybody gives priority to the subjective dimension whilst, at the same time, denying it intellectually. There is such a contradiction, such a flagrant absence of logic in this attitude, it is almost unbelievable! All human beings without exception recognize that the subjective world is the most important for, otherwise, what would be the point of the objective world? What use would it be to anyone to possess all the wealth in the world if he could get no enjoyment out of it? It is the subjective dimension, therefore, which makes everything else worthwhile.

Let me give you another example: when you are lost in admiration at the marvellous achievements of science that have produced the microscopes and telescopes of today, do you ever think of admiring the achievements of nature that have produced your own eyes? Would you be able to see anything through these instruments if you did not have eyes? You are looking at me in astonishment; you had never envisaged the question that way, had you? But I have been deformed, I always look at

The Human Intellect and Cosmic Intelligence

things this way; I say, 'What use would telescopes and microscopes be if we had no eyes?' In fact, I could go even further: our eyes, like any other optical instrument: magnifying glasses, binoculars, field-glasses, etc., belong to the external, visible, objective world and are simply intermediaries. Behind our physical eyes are other eyes, in the brain, and behind the eyes of the brain, lies the spirit. If the spirit were not there, the brain and eyes could function perfectly, but there would be no sight. Even our eyes, which are objective instruments, cannot see if the spirit is not there to see through them. In the order of importance, therefore, it is the spirit that comes first, because it is the spirit that sees through the eyes; telescopes, microscopes, binoculars and so on, come last.

So, there you have just one more proof that the invisible world, the subjective world, the spirit, takes precedence over everything else. And you can apply the same argument to all machines and instruments: planes, rockets, satellites, etc. It is always the spirit that thinks, imagines, calculates and designs. There is always someone who has worked and studied and made discoveries inwardly, in the invisible, subjective dimension. You see? The spirit is always of first importance: without it there would be neither satellites nor rockets nor anything else!

And now, yet another argument: when a crime has been committed, it always involves policemen, lawyers, judges... and sometimes a dog! And what does the dog do? It follows a scent, something that is virtually immaterial (although, to be exact, an odour consists of very subtle material particles), for miles until it finds the criminal who, to be sure, is material and clearly visible! So, working with something that cannot be seen, weighed or measured, the dog follows up a track until it finds the culprit; it is obviously something of a philosopher. It follows the trail of the criminal by a process of philosophical reasoning: speculation, induction, deduction and logical argumentation: 'Given that... since... but... therefore... Q.E.D!' Well, that may make you laugh, but how do judges, lawyers and detectives proceed? By deduction. They argue, 'Since the victim was in such and such a place at a particular time, and that the suspect was there at the same time, etc., etc...', and by following a logical sequence of deductions, they arrive at the truth and condemn or acquit the suspect.

Everybody works in this way, with the help of their intellectual faculties. There is no way of denying that these faculties exist; men are constantly proving their existence by the discoveries that they make with their help. But where do man's intellectual faculties come from? Who gave them to him? Ah, this is where materialists are beaten: they imagine that we are the only beings in the universe to enjoy these faculties, that everything else in the universe is absurd, meaningless, devoid of intelligence, the work of chance. Man has intellectual faculties, he thinks that he is intelligent, but he denies the existence of an Intelligence that has created everything that exists. What about his own ears, with the marvellously delicate elements that go to make up the organ of Corti: was it man who made them? Was it man who created his own eyes, mouth, nose and genitals? And what about the process of gestation: was it man who invented that? To deny the existence of the Intelligence whose hand can be seen in the least little thing around us, in plants, crystals and the movements of the stars, is to say that all existence is founded on the absurd and man is a monster! It seems inconceivable that men, with all their intellectual faculties, should arrive at the conclusion that everything is absurd. Yes, because intelligence should recognize intelligence, not absurdity, nonsense, nothingness.

Intellectuals who adopt a materialistic philosophy are stunted, unnatural monsters, and those who follow them are doomed to end in disaster and fall with them into the abyss. For, to believe in chance is a denial of Cosmic Intelligence and, once one does away with intelligence as the foundation and basis of everything, nothing has meaning or a reason for existing any more; morality and purpose vanish from the scene. From the pedagogical point of view it is the most detestable philosophy because, if human beings are to be educated and led to higher moral and spiritual standards, if they are to be persuaded to accomplish anything worthwhile socially and collectively, they need to know that the universe is governed by intelligence, reason, meaning... that which has always been known as 'God', 'the Lord'. In fact, if none of that actually existed we would have to invent it, for human existence needs a purpose, a destination; without a goal, it can only end in disaster! And all those scientists who think that life is purely fortuitous, a question of chance, will one day be rejected: into the dustbin with them! Yes, because the day will come when all mankind will understand how monstrous a thing materialistic philosophy is. Materialistic philosophers and scientists are a great misfortune for human society, and even if no one else is ready to speak up, I have no hesitation in saying: 'They unleash the forces of the void, they open an abyss before your feet. Don't trust them!' In fact, for the sake of parents, I must add, 'If this is the conclusion that science leads to, then it is not worth sending your children to school!' Yes, I am obliged to speak the truth; they are leading mankind to the grave! To be sure, that is not true of all scientists. Fortunately! There are some who are opposed to these preposterous theories.

And where is the proof that intelligence exists? In the fact that we possess it! We would not have intelligence if it existed nowhere else. We are not capable of creating our own intelligence, it is something that has been given to us; someone gave it to us. Who? That's simple! We only need a little logic, an ability to reason, a little common sense to find the answer. Besides, don't we all use the powers of reasoning that have been given to us? They may be adequate or inadequate, good or bad, but we all use them to form an opinion about life. Why, for instance, do people easily agree that certain people are intelligent while others are stupid? Because we base our judgement on what they do, on their success and the results of their work. When someone is an obvious success in life, we say that he is intelligent. And when someone makes a mess of things and never succeeds in what he undertakes, we agree that it is because he is stupid.

Our conclusions about what is invisible, that is to say, about someone's intelligence and intellectual capacities are based, therefore, on what is visible and tangible. We form an opinion about what we cannot see on the basis of what we can see. Everybody can see your achievements and judge you according to what they see. And since this is how we reason in everyday life, since we judge people to be intelligent or stupid according to the results they achieve, why don't we use the same criteria to reason about the creations of nature? When we see the stars, crystals, plants, mountains and oceans, when we see our own bodies and physical organs, why do we not arrive at the conclusion that an invisible intelligence must exist?

It seems that this argument has never occurred to you. In fact, it seems that you still have not really understood what I am saying. You listen, but without really appreciating this argument at its true worth. Wait! Let me repeat this: since everyone in the world judges the ability of others on the basis of their manifestations, on the basis of what they produce, why don't they do the same in respect to nature? Yes, when you see the achievements of astronomers, mathematicians, physicists and chemists, you are filled with admiration for man and his intelligence, and yet, when you think of the cosmos and the whole universe, you are not moved with wonder and admiration for the intelligence of Him who created works of such sublime, indescribable grandeur and beauty!

Remember the words of the psalmist:
'The heavens declare the glory of God; and the firmament shows His handiwork!'

This is the argument I can give to those who really want to use their reason, to all those who are really sincere and honest.

Obviously, if someone is stubborn – and insincere into the bargain – there is nothing I can do for him! I would be wasting my breath, like the husband of the obstinate woman in the story... She was as stubborn as a mule, she never gave in. When she had got hold of the wrong end of the stick, her husband was very kind and patient and tried to explain things to her, but he never managed to convince her that she was mistaken. One day they had an argument about a pair of scissors; in spite of all the evidence to the contrary, she maintained that a certain piece of cloth had been cut with those scissors. Her husband tried to show her that she was wrong, but nothing he said had any effect; she continued to insist that it had been cut with those scissors. Finally, at the end of his patience, her husband decided that he could not endure such an obstinate wife a minute longer, and threw her into the river, and she, as she was going down for the third time, stuck her arm out of the water and made a gesture, like that, with two fingers, to show that the cloth had been cut with those scissors! What a woman: she was incapable of giving in! Aren't materialistic scientists a little like that woman? In spite of all the evidence against them, they go on repeating, 'Nature is not intelligent; there is no such thing as intelligence in the universe. Everything is the result of chance!' And, like that woman, they are drowning!

Try to understand what I am saying. This is a very simple, logical argument and it shows how blind all those clever people are. They are supposed to be enlightened and learned, and yet they are incapable of arriving at such an obvious conclusion. But why do you suppose that Cosmic Intelligence has given us our powers of reasoning? To guide us and help us to arrive at the truth.

And then there is another thing: for a long time, scientists maintained that life did not exist on the other planets or stars, only on earth. But couldn't they have followed quite a different line of reasoning and said that, since the earth was so tiny that an observer in the constellation of Hercules or Cassiopeia could not even see it, was it plausible to think that life existed on this one tiny speck of dust lost in the vastness of space, and nowhere else in all that multitude of planets and constellations? How unlikely that is! However feeble one's powers of reasoning, it is just not possible to accept such an idea. It is not necessary to be a scientist or an Initiate to know that; it takes no great powers of thought to understand that life must also exist on other planets, although, obviously, under quite different conditions. The fact that, on Mars or anywhere else, there is more or less nitrogen, carbon, oxygen or other gasses than on the earth does not mean that some form of life does not exist. Is it so difficult to understand that Cosmic Intelligence is capable of creating life in conditions that are unknown on earth? Look at a tree: it has no lungs, no intestines and no brain, and yet there are trees that live for thousands of years! It is obvious that it is possible for life to appear and find support in conditions which are not exactly the same as ours. When scientists analysed the composition of certain aerolites, for instance, they discovered minute quantities of carbon and of certain micro-organisms. Life does exist in outer space, therefore. And if it also exists on earth it is because it was brought to earth; it did not appear spontaneously, all on its own; it was brought here from somewhere else. All this will be discovered one day.

So you see, thanks to our intellect and our powers of reasoning, feeble though they may be, thanks to the light we already possess, even if it is no more than a tiny candle, we can discover a great deal. This is obvious from the fact that we have already discovered so much. And if we really knew how to reason, we would also discover the existence of Cosmic Intelligence. 'But I can't see it!' you will object. That is no reason to disbelieve. You cannot see the human intellect either and yet you accept that it exists. We cannot see Cosmic Intelligence, but we have to accept that It exists because the grandeur of Its works speaks for It. What I am telling you today can be a light for all the men and women on earth who seek the truth. They will understand that they had been led into error by people who did not know what they were talking about. A biologist, who can look at the splendour of the human body and still say that everything in nature is the result of chance, does not know what he is talking about; he is both ignorant and blind! And these are the people who get the Nobel Prize! They are people who are a danger to mankind and I certainly don't advise anyone to follow them. The truth is that everything that exists speaks of Divine Intelligence.

And look at the blindness of materialistic philosophers and scientists when it comes to the question of the human soul: they say, 'The soul? No one has ever found one! Man has been auscultated and examined with every sort and kind of instrument and no one has ever seen a soul. Therefore it doesn't exist!' The conclusion is not valid. Have they ever seen life under a microscope? No. Have they ever seen a man's intelligence? Or his thoughts? His consciousness? No, again; and yet they accept that these things exist! But they refuse to accept that the soul exists because they have 'never been able to see one'. Well, all I can say is that, if they have never been able to see the soul, it is not the fault of the soul! And do we have to get rid of it, now, simply because all their instruments have never been able to find it? And they draw the same conclusion with respect to Cosmic Intelligence: they have never actually seen It, therefore It does not exist. What poor reasoning! I warn them: one day, people will turn their backs on them and seek another kind of science, a living, luminous, educational science. They will say, 'This is the truth we've been looking for! We've been led into error and laid waste; our wings have been clipped; we no longer believe in anything; we're heading straight for disaster'. Yes, this materialistic, objective science will be supplanted by another science which will embrace both aspects: the objective and the subjective. Other scientists will make their appearance and bring us a science that gives us the whole picture and, when this happens, man will free himself from all his weaknesses and become an expression of the Deity. So far, man is not much more than a hairy gargoyle, a deformed monster!

In the future, when human beings are no longer content with only the outer aspect, they will live and work in their inner world; they will even be capable of projecting that inner world into the external dimension. They will be capable of condensing all that is most marvellous in the human soul and of giving it material form. They will not even need external objects; they will create whatever they need, themselves. Yes, one day, man will become a true creator. Just as God created the world, man will create his own external world. For the moment, the poor wretch can only bow his head and accept the world in which he finds himself; he no longer has the inner power to improve it or even to stand up to it; he is fashioned by the world around him. If it affords him a few little advantages, he is satisfied, but if it gives him nothing, he dies! He is not in a very enviable position! But in the future, man will be so strong and powerful, he will have such mastery over everything, that the external world will be a reflection of his own inner world. Then he will know splendour, immensity, omnipotence, wealth. But, at the moment, he is nobody! He is obliged to surrender and give way on all fronts; he is at the mercy of the outer world, he can only submit. You can see proof of this when someone who was very rich loses his wealth: it is the end of him, he throws in the sponge and commits suicide. Whereas those who have cultivated a strong inner life say, 'I may have no more money, but I'm still here; I have my gifts and talents and I'm capable of getting all that money back!' This is how someone who has learned to work with his inner world surmounts every difficulty.

There: that was just a few words about today's theme for meditation. It contains a great deal, this theme. In fact, let me tell you that, one day, man will no longer be obliged to talk; his silence, that is to say, his inner life, his thought, will be so intense that it will manifest itself outwardly in the form of colours, projections, perfumes. His only speech will be the power of his inner life. At the moment, he still needs to talk because his inner life is not sufficiently powerful for him to make himself understood without words. In any case, others would be unable to understand him, for they have no inner life, no antennae, no intuition... nothing!

And now you must make up your minds to put the great truths you receive here into practice in your lives for, if you don't actually live and experience them, you will be unable to take them with you and, when you come back again, you will have to start all over again from scratch. Some virtuoso performers make music without any depth of inner feeling; next time they incarnate, in spite of the musical skills they have developed in this life, they will have to learn them all over again. Whereas a musician for whom music has been a living experience, takes his talent with him and, when he comes back to earth, at the age of only five or six, he will be like Mozart, capable of composing masterpieces. Others are mathematical geniuses from their earliest years because they have not been content to study mathematics on the purely intellectual level; they also experienced them in their lives. Perhaps you are wondering how it is possible to have a living experience of mathematics? Well, it would take too long to explain it to you today, but it is possible to experience, to live, to touch, taste and materialize even the most abstract realities, even the realities that are furthest from us. But people don't truly live their lives. They make a feeble attempt to study and express a few things, but they don't live them, so they don't really know them. They are like someone who talks and writes books about love without ever having been in love! Once he falls in love he may well be incapable of writing a book, but he will know, from personal experience, what love is!

And this brings us back to the main point of this lecture, the argument that, since we are capable of judging whether a man is intelligent or not by looking at what he produces, when we look at the splendours of creations we are obliged to conclude that there is a higher Intelligence that presides over the whole of creation. In ancient times, candidates for Initiation were asked, 'Do you believe in the existence of an Intelligence in the universe?' And the doors of the temple were opened to those who believed, with every fibre of their being, in that Intelligence.

But there is something else that I should explain in this connection: why there are some whose lucidity, penetration and clarity of mind continually increase, whereas there are others, on the contrary, in which these qualities continually diminish. The reason is that the first category of beings draws continually on the resources of the infinite ocean of universal Intelligence; they have a relationship with this Intelligence, they believe in It and love It so ardently that, little by little, attracted by that love, It reveals Itself to them. Whereas those who do not believe in It are confined to the limited resources of their own intelligence. They are lost in admiration at their intelligence but, as it is necessarily very limited, it soon reaches the end of its reserves and has nothing left to offer. This is the explanation. Sooner or later, those who reject or deny the existence of this Intelligence, will lose their light: their memory, their lucidity, their common sense... all these things will abandon them. They may have devoured whole libraries full of books, but they are destined to end in senility! Whereas the others are permanently in touch with Cosmic Intelligence and that Intelligence is drawn to them and reveals many things to them. Yes, Cosmic Intelligence is ready to reveal all Its treasures to those who love It. There, that's all; each one of you can take the path of his choice: the path of materialistic scientists and philosophers, or that of the Initiates and great Masters, of those who have really understood.

The Human Intellect and Cosmic Intelligence

The secret of true intelligence is to understand, to feel and then to act in accordance with that broad, vast, profound understanding and that sensation which never deceives. I told you, one day, that true intelligence was intuition, for intuition does not need to study or calculate; intuitive understanding is instantaneous, it sees the truth, penetrates a situation in a flash and informs you of its findings at once. I don't know how dictionaries define intuition, but in my definition it is, at one and the same time, understanding and sensation. Intuition enables us to feel and understand something at once. It is a higher form of intelligence, therefore, and it possesses the primary indispensable element: life. And in situations in which others scratch their heads and wonder what to do next, he who possesses this intelligence, and who loves and admires and believes in it, understands the situation at a glance. Yes, once one has begun to discover reality as it truly exists, with its two faces, objective and subjective, one is amazed when one realizes that others cannot see any of that, although it is all so simple! It remains for you, now, to accept the existence of that Intelligence which manifests Itself throughout the universe and fashions everything that exists; accept It, love It and seek It. If you do this you will see for yourselves all the transformations that It is capable of producing within you, not only in your brain but in your whole being.

Seek out this Cosmic Intelligence, love It and beg It to come to you for It will give you a true vision of reality. And believe me, my dear brothers and sisters, that is true wealth: to see the exact reality of things.

The Bonfin, 12 September 1971

Chapter Nine

THE SOLAR PLEXUS AND THE BRAIN

I

Some of you are probably surprised that I sometimes say that God is so far away and inaccessible that it is impossible to communicate with Him and, at other times, I say just the opposite: that God is so close and accessible that one can almost touch Him. Which of these statements is true? Am I contradicting myself? No, actually, there is no contradiction involved.

On the one hand it is true that God is so powerful that anyone who approached Him without being as pure as the Cherubim and Seraphim would be struck down and reduced to dust. High voltage electricity can give you a faint notion of this: if you touch a naked power line you will be killed instantly by electrocution. And what is high voltage electricity compared to the power of God! But electricity is a language that can help us to reflect. Yes, even if God is so powerful as to be totally inaccessible, even if we are too weak and imperfect to tolerate being in His presence, we can still communicate with Him. The entire angelic hierarchy forms a link between Heaven and earth and there is nothing to prevent the life that God showers on us from reaching us, or even from reaching the centre of the earth and the depths of the oceans. But this takes intermediaries or messengers and, gradually, as this divine life moves further and further from the Source, it condenses and coagulates to the point of becoming almost tangible.

The light, heat and life of our daily experience are only a very feeble reflection of true light, true heat and true life. Behind the light of the sun is the light of God, but we can have no direct knowledge of it, any more than we can have direct knowledge of His warmth, His love or His life, that is to say, of the most intense form of life. God is unknowable, utterly beyond our grasp and yet, at the same time, He is so close that He almost touches us, but in a very remote, tenuous form. You must not think that the light of the sun is the true light of God. It is a reflection of that true light, but only a very faint reflection. We are incapable of knowing or comprehending that other light; it is so subtle and powerful that it is as darkness to us, and even to many other spirits far more highly evolved than us.

Initiatic Science tells us that light issued from darkness. In the beginning was chaos, unorganized matter, the *hyle* of the ancient Greeks. Primeval chaos is represented by a circle, a zero; symbolically, the circle represents the infinite, inanimate matter. But it is very difficult, almost impossible, in fact, for the intellect to grasp such notions, and philosophers and scientists who try to understand everything with their intellects fail miserably. The brain can understand the theoretical aspect, to be sure, but it has not been given the power truly to comprehend things, that is to say, to feel, taste and experience them.

As a matter of fact, it is often said that it is the heart that understands, and people speak of 'the intelligence of the heart'. Even the Gospels refer to the heart as being the organ of understanding. But what heart is this? Surely not the physical organ that pumps blood through our bodies? No, the true heart, the Initiatic heart is the solar plexus; this is the organ that feels, understands and grasps the great cosmic truths. The brain is only capable of discussing things, of writing and talking and blustering; it is incapable of forming a clear idea of things. This is what we see in the world of the fifth race of man: everyone teaches, lectures and writes books without really understanding, because true understanding is not within the possibilities of the

The Solar Plexus and the Brain

brain. Things can only be understood when they become a vital experience, an experience of our whole being.

The solar plexus controls all the functions of the physical body; respiration, elimination, nutrition, growth and the circulatory system all depend on the solar plexus. And it is the solar plexus which created and continues to nourish the brain. Yes, the brain is the product, the offspring of the solar plexus. This is why the solar plexus feeds the brain and keeps it supplied with everything it needs. If it ceases to do so a person becomes drowsy and incapable of activity, or he gets a headache and cannot think any more.

The brain is not cut off from the solar plexus, but it cannot always take advantage of its aid, because it has not yet learned how to communicate with it. As I have already explained, the solar plexus is a brain, but a brain in reverse, for in the brain the grey matter is on the outside and the white matter on the inside, whereas in the solar plexus it is the opposite. The grey matter, which is composed of nerve cells, is what enables man to think, while the white matter, composed of nerve fibres, enables him to feel. Thanks to its outer layer of white matter, therefore, the solar plexus feels all that goes on in the body, in every single cell; this is why it is perpetually engaged in restoring order and balance. The brain feels nothing until things have reached very serious proportions, and even then it doesn't know what to do about it. If your heart beats too fast or too slowly, or if you have a stomach ache, the brain can do nothing about it: in any case, that is not its job! But if you give the solar plexus the conditions it needs to function correctly, it can soon put everything right. It possesses an extraordinary store of pharmaceutical products and, as it is in contact with every cell in every organ of your body, it can intervene wherever necessary. It is far better equipped, therefore, than the brain. But this has never been properly explained, even by medical science.

It is also by means of the solar plexus that man maintains contact with the ocean of universal life for, in contrast to the brain, the solar plexus is linked to the whole cosmos. Actually, communication between the brain and the cosmos is not impossible but, at the moment, the brain is still insufficiently developed, for it was formed only very recently; the solar plexus has existed far longer. The brain developed at a relatively late date in animals, and even later in men. In fact the brain of an ant, for instance, is far more highly organized than that of a man, because ants developed much earlier than men! It is astonishing to compare the brain of an ant and that of a man and to see how perfectly ants have managed to organize their minute brains. The human brain is still not fully organized, but this will come, for its mission is to record the totality of knowledge and to conceive great and wonderful things. But, I repeat, the one in charge at the moment, the one who controls and commands all the others, is the solar plexus, in conjunction with the Hara centre which is situated a little lower down.

Westerners are working towards their own destruction because the greater part of their activities are cerebral: they overload their brains with their studies, calculations and burdens of all kinds. The brain is not designed to stand up to so much strain, and much of the nervous ill-health so prevalent today stems from this overload. If people knew how to divide the burden more evenly between the solar plexus and the brain, they would never be tired. Why? Because the solar plexus never tires; it is an almost inexhaustible reservoir. But someone who lives foolishly disturbs the proper functioning of his solar plexus and then he feels constricted and impeded in his work and nervously exhausted. How many times I have already heard the complaint: 'Master, I feel all tight here!' Of course! Their solar plexus has seized up. They live stupidly and they are destroying the one element in their system on which all the rest depends.

There are ways, of course, of communicating directly with one's solar plexus and ordering – or beseeching – it to remedy something that has gone wrong. This is a science that will be studied in the future. For the moment, however, it is not really possible to communicate with one's solar plexus; it has its own independent way of life and there is not much man can do about it. The most he can do is influence it indirectly until such time as he can do so directly. And how can he influence it indirectly? By living a pure, sensible, luminous life in harmony with the whole universe. That kind of life will influence his plexus and free it from its constraints and, when it is given a free hand, it puts things right in no time at all, for it is extremely powerful. It is even capable of changing the form of your body.

How often, in my lectures, I have told you that you must rely on the way you live more than on anything else. Nothing is more important than this: the way you live will always be the key to all the rest. But you think that it is ineffectual, whereas what you eat and drink, your clothes, the house you live in, the machines you use... all these external things you consider to be of paramount importance. Oh, of course, coffee, wine, stimulants and tranquillizers, the company of a pretty girl, travel, etc., etc., all these things are exciting and extremely effective, there is no doubt about that! But if someone says that you must think about the way you live... about changing the way you live... what a bore! And how disappointing! You cannot see that it gives you any results! Well, that is the reasoning of someone who has not lived long enough to see for himself how these laws operate but, in the past, there have been men who lived a very long time and had every opportunity to observe people and events and reach the conclusion that, in the long run, it is the way one lives that is the most important and most effective remedy. External means are effective and rapid only on the surface: they always leave some adverse secondary effects, some broken crockery, some unexpected debts to be paid... the situation only becomes more and more inextricable!

But where will you find someone who talks about the way you live? It will certainly not be either the doctor or the pharmacist: They will tell you, 'Swallow this; it will make you feel better!' No one considers the way you live as having any bearing on your health, except the great Initiates, because they have suffered and understood. But who listens to them? People act according to their passing sensations and never think of the consequences. But I insist – and whether you believe me or not, I shall go on insisting – that the only thing that matters is the way you live! For me, this is an absolute truth. In fact, if something unpleasant happens to me, I tell myself, 'I know why I'm in this state; it's because my way of living is not yet divine.' I do not try to put the blame on anything or anyone else, whereas most human beings accuse their wives, their children, their neighbours, world events, the government and, above all, the Lord! It never, never occurs to them that the cause of all their difficulties and distress could be their own way of living.

I am well aware that what I am saying will not be well received. It is too foreign to you; it does not correspond with your habitual way of looking at things. But whether I enjoy it or not I am obliged to tell you this. Whenever something unpleasant happens to you, if you looked for the cause with real sincerity, you would find that it lay in the fact that you don't live in the right way; in other words, that you don't think, feel or behave in the right way. If you lived properly you would not have so many difficulties and so much inner torment. Yes, if you delude yourself into thinking that you are perfect, even though you are bogged down in difficulties of all kinds, it simply means that you are incapable of reasoning correctly. Make up your minds, immediately, to make the way you live your only criterion, and you will see that all the rest will become much clearer.

And if you ask me whether I myself live as I should, I shall have to say, in all sincerity, 'If I compare myself with many other people whose lives I have observed: yes, I live a magnificent life. But if I compare my life to that of divinities, I can see that I still have a lot of work to do.' Because there are many different degrees of life. If your thoughts are very luminous, if you love everything and everyone in the world and work tirelessly for good, one fine day, when you have moved on to another level, other work, of such splendour as you could never have imagined, will be disclosed to you. Whatever you have done up to then was good, to be sure; in comparison with what the rest of the world does, it was good; but you will find out that there are other, more perfect kinds of activity.

This is the truth; and to tell you this in no way diminishes me. If I compare myself with an ant, of course, I am an elephant; but if I compare myself with the Cherubim and Seraphim, I am an ant... or perhaps a flea! And don't burn the blanket just because this flea bothers you!

The Bonfin, 9 August 1970

II

I want to speak to you again, today, about the relationship between the solar plexus and the brain, for it is important for you to realize what a vast and crucial question this is and what a wealth of complexities it involves.

How do the solar plexus and the brain relate to each other? They are the two poles: the one masculine and emissive and the other, feminine and receptive. This polarity is reflected in every sphere of nature. Take a case that you are all familiar with, that of certain married couples: the husband spends his time working to earn money to buy clothes for his wife. She is elegant, expensively dressed and enormously attractive, whilst her wretched husband slaves away for her sake in his dirty old working clothes.

You are certainly familiar, also, with the experiment of the Crooke's tube (See the following figure): when an electric current is applied between two electrodes in the tube, the cathode emits a flow of electrons in the direction of the anode. The cathode remains dark but the anode lights up.

The Solar Plexus and the Brain

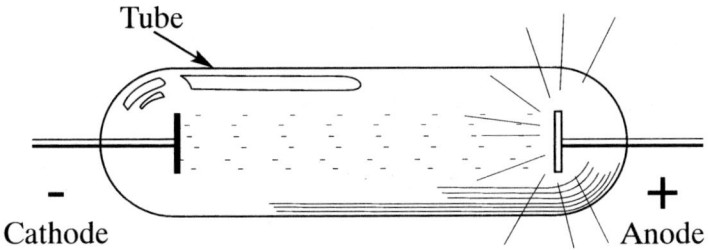

Crooke's Tube

This is an excellent illustration of the relationship between the masculine and feminine principles. Everywhere, throughout the whole of nature, these two principles are at work. As I have already told you, this is the Initiatic Science which Melchizedek revealed to Abraham: the existence of the two principles and the manner in which they work together, manifesting themselves in a multitude of different forms throughout the universe.

The brain manifests itself, speaks, issues its orders, shouts and gesticulates and generally makes a fuss. But does the initiative actually come from the brain? No, it is the solar plexus that supplies the brain with energy, but without calling attention to itself. It is always there, but behind the scenes; so quiet and discreet that no one ever suspects its presence. The solar plexus is the humble, hard-working husband... although, in point of fact its role is feminine; it is the foster-mother, the infinitely wealthy, inexhaustible reservoir of nature. And the brain? The brain was formed by the solar plexus, it is its child. Or, if you prefer, the brain is the husband, another kind of husband, one who is always holding forth, arguing, issuing anathemas in all directions! You have to understand these changes of polarity. As a matter of fact, Hindus say that the home of Siva (the dynamic, destructive principle) is the brain, and that the brain, that is to say, the intellect, the mental dimension, is the destroyer of reality.

The brain is active and dynamic but it tires very quickly if the solar plexus fails to subsidize it regularly. For this reason, before activating the brain, before concentrating or meditating, a disciple should do a preliminary work with his solar plexus. The brain is capable of great things, but on condition that the solar plexus keeps it supplied with energy. There are days when, in spite of your efforts, you cannot seem to arouse your brain from its somnolence; this means that there is some obstacle in the way, the solar plexus has failed to supply it with the elements it needs. And then, on other days, intellectual work comes easily because the plexus has given the brain the elements it needs. The source, therefore, the cause, is the solar plexus, and the brain is like a screen which manifests and expresses whatever is projected by the plexus. It is exactly what happens in the cinema, with the difference, of course, that, in the cinema, the masculine principle is the cameraman (or his projector) who throws pictures onto the screen, and the screen is the feminine principle, the matter onto which the spirit projects forces and energies. As you see: yet another change of polarity!

When you look at an object, the image of it is reversed in your eye; then, when that image is transmitted to the brain, it is reversed again and you see it as it is. If you look at your reflection in a mirror, you see that the right side of your body has crossed over to the left, and the left to the right. If you look at the reflection of trees and houses in the water of a lake, you will see them upside-down: what is on top is seen at the bottom, and what is at the bottom is seen at the top. This phenomenon of reversal and crossing over is one of the great mysteries of creation.

If one studies the way in which the two principles operate in men and women, one sees that man is active and emissive on the physical plane, whereas woman is receptive. On the astral plane, however, man becomes receptive and woman emissive.

The Solar Plexus and the Brain

On a higher level again, that of the mental plane, man is once again emissive and woman receptive, and so on; from one plane to the next, the polarity crosses over and is reversed. According to Hindu philosophy, Kundalini, which is a feminine force, is an active principle which takes the initiative in travelling upwards to unite with Siva, the masculine principle, who remains motionless in the brain. In Christianity, the symbol of the cross also represents this reversal of processes and activities in nature. Christians have never understood the profound symbolism of the cross, which has existed for thousands and thousands of years. It was not Christianity that invented the cross. It can be found in all religions throughout the world in some form or another, because there is a tremendous science hidden in this phenomenon of crossing over.

To my mind, the most meaningful form of cross is the three-dimensional cross, consisting of twenty-two surfaces which correspond to the twenty-two letters of the Hebrew alphabet. Yes, if you place five cubes in a certain pattern: one in the centre, one on top, one below, one to the left and one to the right, you will get a cross with twenty-two square surfaces (See the following figure). The five cubes represent the five elements. But what is this fifth element? One never hears any mention of it. Well, what does quintessence mean? Just that: the *quinta essentia*, the fifth essence. The quintessence of something is its fifth essence or element, a subtle element which dwells in and impregnates the four elements of earth, water, air and fire.

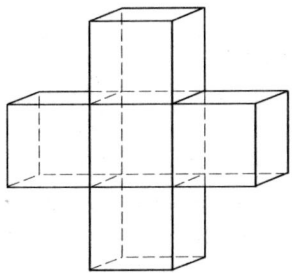

A disciple who practises meditation must realize that his brain cannot carry the whole burden alone, otherwise it will be exhausted and an unhealthy tension or even a serious nervous imbalance can result. He must call on his solar plexus. This is why, as soon as you feel that your brain is beginning to seize up, I advise you to massage your solar plexus with a circular anti-clockwise motion. In a very few minutes you will feel that your thought is once more flowing freely and you can get back to work. You have to learn to share out the work between the brain and the solar plexus just as, in true marriage, the husband and wife live in harmony and share the work between them. In these conditions the brain will be able to manifest the powers stored in the plexus. The solar plexus contains, in its archives, all the knowledge acquired ever since the most remote past, and it is the task of the brain to retrieve and express this knowledge. The brain is simply an instrument designed to bring to light all the treasures buried in the depths of our being and, incidentally, this is why the solar plexus is placed well below the level of the brain.

The Initiates of India, the Rishis, who possessed this science, placed Brahmâ, the Creator, in man's entrails: in the solar plexus. To western minds this does not seem very respectful! But, since the Rishis acknowledged the Creator as the all-powerful, all-glorious One to whom all other divinities were subservient, would they have placed Him on such a lowly level if they did not have a good reason for doing so? What reason? The answer escapes us. And why did they place Visnu in the lungs and heart? And why is Siva located in the brain, as though it were Siva who personified intelligence and wisdom? There is a great mystery here, a secret wisdom which was known to the Sages of ancient Hinduism. To be sure, Brahmâ is not exactly the feminine principle but, in this context, He represents both spirit and matter, the Creator and the Supreme Mother, the Primordial Being from whom all else proceeds.

What I have tried to do, today, in talking to you about the brain and the solar plexus, is to give you some more examples

The Solar Plexus and the Brain

of the activity of the two principles, masculine and feminine. These two principles are to be found everywhere, even in wheat and grapes, even in the human countenance. Hinduism represents them in the form of the linga ⚲ and, in the Hebrew alphabet, they are symbolized by the letter Shin שׁ which takes the shape of a boat with a mast, or of the head and wings of a bird. And, when a man raises his two arms in prayer, he resembles the Shin, the linga; his physical attitude symbolizes the two principles.

In the previous lecture, I told you that the solar plexus was also a brain, but reversed. The white matter of the solar plexus communicates with the white matter of the brain, and the grey matter of the plexus with the grey matter of the brain. We see here yet another reversal of position, a crossing over, and this crossing over takes place at the level of the neck. This is why, if you feel that communications are not getting through as they should, it can help to massage your neck in the region of the cervical vertebrae, and get the currents flowing again between the solar plexus and the brain. And if you squeeze a person's neck too violently you can kill him, because the life flowing from the solar plexus cannot get through to the brain. This gives you some idea of the importance of these nerve centres. But medical science has never studied the crossover that takes place on the level of the neck (and which puts the left side of the body under the control of the right hemisphere of the brain and vice versa), from the point of view of its cosmic correspondences.

When a disciple meditates, he must learn to make contact with his solar plexus and share his activity equally between the plexus and the brain. When he learns to concentrate on his solar plexus with an attitude of love, he will be able to tap its immense resources of energy and direct them to the brain.

I have probably already told you about how I berated a well-known author who had ridiculed an esoteric teaching in one of his books, because it advised its adepts to concentrate on their navel. I really told him off! I asked him, 'Have you ever studied the question?' 'No', he replied. 'Then you know nothing about it. You scoff at people who focus their attention on their navel, and yet you know nothing about the vital energies concealed in that region or where this tradition comes from.' I showed him how ignorant he was on the subject and advised him not to write about questions like that, otherwise he would find himself the butt of other, more enlightened critics who would put him in his place. Why do people meddle in things they know nothing about?

This practice of concentrating on the region of the navel, which harbours centres as vital as the solar plexus and the Hara centre, has a very ancient history: it was developed by Initiates who knew the human structure, who knew how man had been put together in the workshops of the Lord. As a matter of fact, I could give you the names of several very remarkable Christian authors who have written about this practice and about the sensations and revelations they obtained as a result. Hundreds of years ago, therefore, some Christians already knew these things. Of course, I realize that all kinds of bizarre customs and beliefs have been invented by ignorant or unbalanced people and tagged on to this practice, but that is no reason to reject it out of hand. The practice of concentrating on the Hara centre has very profound meaning.

If man is to manifest himself fully, there must be harmonious communication between the solar plexus and the brain. The brain is simply a kind of screen on which all kinds of images can be projected; insofar as what we might call 'the brain in the belly' projects pictures correctly onto the screen of the other brain, man becomes truly active. And, here again, we find an example of a phenomenon which exists in every area of life. A young man is taken under the wing of an elderly millionaire, who gives him money and takes care of his education and, having completed his university studies, he becomes an eminent scientist or artist. If he had never had anyone to help him, he would have been a nobody all his life, for he had neither the money nor the opportunity to develop his talents. There have always been very talented people who failed to accomplish anything because they never met someone who could help them.

When one studies the lives of military or scientific geniuses, for example, one often finds that the source of their success was a woman, a loving, generous woman, who remained discreetly in the background, but who was always there with the encouragement, consolation and inspiration they needed. If they achieved some kind of success it was thanks to this discreet, hidden centre. And on the contemporary political scene, do you know who is behind each minister or Head of State? If there were no one in the background to encourage and support them, they would not last more than a day! Behind every public figure, there is always someone who pulls the strings, but one never knows who: it is a mystery. If a certain minister is very powerful and at the peak of his career today, it is often because others are behind him and have used publicity and the press to promote his cause. And if these same people decided to destroy his career, it would be all over within twenty-four hours! It is always like that: there is always one dark, invisible centre and another, beside it, which shines thanks to the unseen presence of the dark centre.

I have already spoken to you, a long time ago, about the 'dark sun' from which our own sun receives its energy. The dark sun, which never stops giving, is the masculine principle, and our sun which receives the energy that enables it to shine, represents the feminine principle. And not only does it shine, it also smiles! Yes, look at the drawings children always make of the sun, with a smile from ear to ear! The sun is always smiling! I am not going to tell you that I have actually seen the dark sun, but I have seen it inwardly. It is always there; it exists and, without it, there would be no bright, visible sun. It is the story of the cathode and the anode all over again; it is a Crooke's tube, stretched to the dimensions of the universe.

How clear and simple it is! Everywhere, absolutely everywhere, we see the two principles. Would you like me to give you yet another example? Take that of a tree: a tree has roots, a trunk and branches. It is the roots that send energy up the trunk to the branches so that leaves, flowers and fruit can appear. You cannot see the roots, but if you were to do away with them, all the things that you can see would disappear also! All visible things are the fruit of something that is invisible and hidden deep down beneath the surface. In man, the solar plexus represents the roots of a tree, and his trunk and members the trunk and branches of the tree. Like a tree, man has roots, a trunk and branches and, in the brain, flowers and fruit. The roots of the brain are the solar plexus which is, therefore, the more important of the two, for it is always the roots that are most important; if anything goes wrong with them the whole tree dies. You see? Yet another irrefutable argument: if you cut off the roots of a tree, you kill the tree.

From the solar plexus come the pictures that are projected onto the screen of the brain. Whether they are good or evil, they are projected. And let me give you yet another impressive argument: What is a man? A man is the one who projects the pictures or films. And a woman? A woman is the screen. And a child? A child is the film, the picture. But a woman is a strange kind of screen, for she condenses the images projected onto her by man so well that they materialize and acquire a life of their own. But I must wait for another occasion to explain all this to you. In any case, you can already see that it is always the same law: solar plexus and brain; man and woman... And the child is the projected image which the woman materializes: to begin with, the child is nothing more than a quintessence, but then the woman's action materializes it and makes it tangible.

A few minutes ago I told you that the image of the objects we see is upside down on the screen of the retina. Why is this?

Then the image is reversed and we perceive it right side up. The same pattern can be seen in men and women. On the physical plane the woman is at the bottom and the man at the top. On the astral plane it is the reverse: the woman is at the top and the man below. On the mental plane, the positions are the same as on the physical plane. And so on... Why has nature designed things in this way?

The main thing to remember about what we have been saying today is that, if you work exclusively with your brain, you will very rapidly exhaust yourself. You must learn to distribute the work-load fairly between the two centres: that which is down below, in the belly, and that which is above, in the brain. You will find true equilibrium only if you do this. It is a law of mechanics: if you want the two pans of a scales to balance, you must not load only one of them. You have to put the same weight into each pan.

The Bonfin, 19 September 1970

Chapter Ten

THE HARA CENTRE

I

You are in an Initiatic school where you are being taught to see, feel, understand and taste things, that is to say, to discover the meaning of life, and this is more important than anything else. That is why I ask you to be more attentive and to help me in what I am trying to do for you. When you understand me and accept the points of view that I explain, you will be able to climb much more rapidly to the peaks from which you will see the world as a whole. And it is precisely this, the coherent unity of the world, that gives meaning to everything that exists.

At the moment, all the different elements you possess are jumbled up inside you. There are plenty of planks, nails, bricks, cement and glass lying about, but they have not yet been assembled into a building; you still have to learn to put all these materials together and build your palace... or temple. In the world you are given quantities of materials and told to make what you can of them! So you go on amassing more and more disparate items but you are never satisfied, because nobody ever teaches you what to do with them. All you have is a stock of separate elements... and that is called culture and civilization! To be sure, all these things could be put to good use, but no one ever explains what to do or how to do it. Whereas, here, in an Initiatic school, it is your work that counts. Obviously, you also need materials, but the important thing is to know how to fit them all together and what design to follow in doing so.

Henceforth, you can help me in my work by understanding what we are doing here. And stop comparing me to prominent lecturers, intellectuals and scientists! To be sure, they can give you as much material as you want, so much, in fact, that you will be crushed to death beneath the weight of it, whereas, here, you will be given next to nothing. No, but you will learn to be alive, and that is much better. Here, you are given life and, as the days go by, I see you becoming more and more expressive, active, dynamic, conscious, resolute and orientated. It is possible that some of you are losing a little weight, but your life, your spirit is gaining! When it is only matter that gains, it is not so good, but when both matter and spirit gain, that is excellent. If a man is too skinny and weak, as thin as a rake, that is not good either; others will say, 'Oh, him? Pooh! The first breath of wind will blow him away!'

When I was in India I was astonished to see that many saddhus and yogis had very big bellies although they ate hardly anything! And why do all the statues of Buddha or other sages portray them with a generous paunch? To be sure, in some people, a big belly is a sign of materialism, grossness and sensuality. But in an Initiate, it is a sign of power and strength, an indication of the spiritual reserves he has accumulated thanks to years of special breathing exercises. Yes, for prolonged breathing exercises develop this region of the body in which are stored certain elements which enable him to heal sickness and disintegrate harmful influences. A pot-belly, therefore, can be the result either of a materialistic or of a spiritual way of life. If a man's face reveals that he is only interested in eating, drinking and sleeping then, of course, his corpulence is a bad sign. But if he is pure, clairvoyant and intelligent, then his stoutness shows that he has substantial reserves which he can call upon to heal others and do a great many things which a thin, weedy little fellow cannot do, because he lacks the resources.

The Hara Centre

Look at the Japanese: some of them are enormously fat, and yet they are very supple and strong and also very intelligent. The explanation is that they develop what they call the *Hara* centre. This is the centre situated just four centimetres below the navel. In Japanese, the word hara means belly, and the expression *hara-kiri*, which we have all heard of, means to commit suicide by opening the belly. According to Japanese sages, the Hara is man's life-centre, his centre of gravity, the universal centre; and he who concentrates on it and develops it to the full, becomes tireless and invincible.

It is the exaggerated, unbalanced activity of the brain that fatigues people. A great many of the problems of our day come from the fact that people in the West have upset the balance: instead of finding their centre of gravity, their life-centre in the Hara centre, they find it in the brain which, by rights, represents the periphery of man. Too much thinking, too many cares, too much cerebral activity have unbalanced man. This is why, when his system receives a shock of any kind he is so easily knocked off balance: his centre of gravity which would normally remedy the situation is not functioning correctly. If one knew how to concentrate on the Hara centre and develop it correctly, one could afford to do a great deal of intellectual work without ever being tired. All those who have really worked to develop their Hara centre are remarkable for their extraordinary equilibrium. This is a science that will be much developed in the future: the science of how to work with the brain and the Hara centre.

Of course, there is a problem here for Westerners, because the belly and sexual organs, all the lower parts of the physical body have always been considered unworthy of a spiritual role. Whereas the upper regions were considered very noble and distinguished! This is why Westerners attach so much importance to the brain. In spite of the fact that this lower centre has an essential role to play in both the physical and the spiritual life, nobody is interested in developing it, nobody is interested in anything but the brain. I don't mean that you should neglect the brain: not at all! To be well-balanced, you have to develop both aspects, for the centre and the periphery are both important in their own way. The centre represents the sun, the periphery the planets; and since living creatures exist on the planets also, the periphery is important and must not be neglected.

In my lectures I have always insisted on the importance of the centre and for years, when I spoke of the 'centre', I almost always meant the Supreme Centre, God Himself, the First Cause, the Fountainhead. I have never told you before that, in the physical body, man's true centre was there, just below the navel. This centre is mentioned in many esoteric books, but often in very different ways. For example, in his book, 'The Twelve Keys', the renowned alchemist, Basil Valentine, speaks of descending to the centre of the earth to seek the Philosophers' Stone. He says: *'Visita interiora terrae. Rectificando invenies occultum lapidem, veram medicinam'*, which means: 'Visit the bowels of the Earth; if you rectify you will find the hidden Stone, the true medicine.' If you take the first letter of each of the Latin words: *Visita Interiora Terrae* etc., you will find that they form the word VITRIOLUM. In fact, of course, Valentine was not talking about descending into the centre of the planet Earth, but into our own earth, our own physical body, for it is there that we shall find materials, treasure and wealth...

I have studied the Hindu pantheon, with all its multitudes of deities (although, as a matter of fact, it is really not necessary to study all of them; there are so many it is impossible to sort them all out!), and amongst all these divinities, the most important are Brahmâ, Visnu and Siva. The Hindu sacred scriptures say that Brahmâ resides in the belly, Visnu in the region of the heart and lungs and Siva in the brain. Why should Brahmâ, the Creator, be said to reside in the belly? If the belly is so despicable, and the brain, on the contrary, so noble, one would have thought that the Hindu mystics would have assigned Brahmâ to the brain.

No, it is Siva who is associated with the brain, because Siva is the great destroyer. Brahmâ is the Creator; Visnu the preserver, he who repairs, sustains and nourishes, while Siva is the destroyer. And if Siva has been identified with the brain, it is because the brain – that is to say the lower mental body – divides, dissects, and disintegrates; it is the destroyer of reality; it gives men a false picture of reality. But then, how do Initiates learn? They learn by having recourse, not exclusively to the brain, like most Westerners, but also to their other God-given faculties.

One day, when I was very young, the Master Peter Deunov told me that, in his spiritual work, a disciple had to descend into his own bowels, because that was where God dwelt. This intrigued me for a very long time because, of course, the Master did not explain what he meant. When he told us something, he expected us to puzzle our heads over it and work it out for ourselves! He was very unlike me: I take a spoon and say, 'Open your mouths!' But not he: he was very wise; he let us dig out the meaning for ourselves. He never talked for hours on end, as I do. He wanted his brothers and sisters to do their own work, for that was the best way for them to strengthen themselves. Whereas I have a tendency to make you weaker and more reliant, because I want to give you everything. I know that it would take you years – centuries, in fact – to find these truths for yourselves, and I want to spare you the need to waste so much time and, perhaps, find nothing. Yes, but I admit that it is not a very educational method, for human beings never value something that they obtain too easily. This is why the things I reveal have no effect on you. Oh, well; it doesn't matter; it's my loss!

When one looks at human beings, one sees that the belly is the centre in which life is created. Yes, the source of life is there, in the belly. Even the Gospels say, 'Out of his belly will flow rivers of living water'. Why 'out of his belly'? Why not out of the brain or the lungs? What makes the belly so special that living waters should flow from it? It is because Brahmâ, the Creator, dwells here. But in order to feel and experience his presence and communicate with him it takes years and years of hard work. He is there, but we don't feel his presence or benefit from it in any way because we are too busy working with Siva. While I was in India, I was struck by a fact which is familiar to everyone who knows India, and that is that only a few temples are dedicated to Brahmâ; more are dedicated to Visnu, and many more still to Siva. Why is this? Is it from fear of Siva the destroyer? Do men honour him in order to appease him? Whereas no one needs to be afraid of Brahmâ, the Creator; there is no danger that he would ever harm anyone; perhaps that is why he is neglected!

Westerners are not even aware of the existence of the Hara centre. They ought to have learned at least this from the Japanese. But whether it be with the Japanese or the Tibetans, Hindus or Egyptians, these great truths are handed on from one generation to the next, and from one people to another. Even primitive Christianity possessed some elements of this knowledge and used it in certain methods of meditation. And nowadays, certain occultists teach how to concentrate on one's navel. They do not know that, in actual fact, the most important centre – in conjunction, of course, with the solar plexus and the centre situated in the sexual organs – is just a little below the navel. To be sure, the navel has an important function: I remember that, when I was a child, I often saw my Mother healing somebody by massaging their navel. Even now, in spite of her age, she still heals a lot of people: she tells them to lie down, uncovers their navel and, dipping her finger wrapped in a handkerchief into some ashes, massages it with a circular motion. She says that there is a vital point in the navel and that, if it is displaced, the whole organism begins to deteriorate. With her massage she puts this point back in place. I remember that she cured me with this method when I was young. Of course, if you told doctors that, they would laugh you to scorn for believing in such a barbaric, archaic method. Let them laugh! Do they always cure people with their 'modern' methods?

If I decided to speak to you, today, about these different centres, it was in the hope of getting you to understand their sacredness. The fact that the belly has always been seen as something rather grotesque is no reason for you not to take what I say seriously. In any case, it is part of my programme to talk to you, one day, about the different exercises and experiments you can do with the Hara centre in order to purify yourselves and reach a state of perfect balance, for this is the way to become truly tireless, strong and powerful. When meditating, some spiritualists place both hands on their belly; this is because they are concentrating on the Hara centre in order to stimulate its energies and get them to flow through and nourish their whole body. You can do this, too. If, for example, you feel that your brain is overworked and beginning to seize up, put your intellectual work aside and concentrate on this centre. After only a few minutes, your brain will feel restored and you can get back to work.

You must remember, though, that there is a danger: if you are not capable of working with the Hara centre in a spirit of purity, abnegation and disinterestedness, if, instead of undertaking this work for the good of mankind, you do it for personal gain, to obtain power or prestige etc., you will find that other centres will be aroused. This is the terrible thing: if you are not very careful, it is not the Hara centre that will be stimulated but other, diabolical centres, and you will be dragged down by underground currents from which you will be unable to escape. If I have never spoken about the Hara centre before, it is because you must prepare yourselves before experimenting with this kind of exercise. Once you are prepared, you can explore these depths without danger, for this is the abyss, the veritable underworld of human nature.

To be sure, psychoanalysts have explored some areas of the subconscious, but they are still a long way from understanding all the mysteries of human nature and they do not know that the Hara centre, which is buried in the depths of the subconscious, is also linked with the superconsciousness. When the Initiates speak of making both ends meet, that is to say, of joining the head and the tail of the serpent, they are saying that we must join this lower centre to that other centre above, on the top of the head. But how can you hope to accomplish anything worthwhile in these perilous lower regions if you have not prepared yourselves beforehand, thanks to all the methods that I have given you. You would have to turn back in confusion... or worse, far worse. Try to understand me: in the spiritual life, too, you have to follow a programme. You must begin by purifying and strengthening yourself and then, when you feel ready to do so, you can venture into the lower regions: this is an experience that lies ahead of you, but you must not launch into it too soon.

Children are formed in their mother's womb and, since life is all that is most sacred, surely the place in which it has elected to begin is not something shameful? Human beings have never studied the design of Cosmic Intelligence to find out why It chose this spot. The first thing to do is to correct all our false notions and get back to an understanding of the sacredness of the belly... and of the sexual organs. When one hears some of the things people say about them, and all the dirty jokes... And it is these organs that produce life! Your mouth cannot produce life, and nor can your nose, your ears or your brain. Only the organs that people think of as shameful have been given the mission to perpetuate the human race. You will say, 'This is scandalous! When you praise these organs you are encouraging all those who lead a life of debauchery and think about nothing but sexual pleasure!' No, not at all; I am simply showing you the profound, sacred, magic side of things; this does not mean that I am encouraging you to do anything stupid. Don't imagine that I am urging you to indulge your sensuality. What I am interested in is to see how the Intelligence of Nature works and why it creates things as it does. Of course, I know why men were led to consider the regions of the belly and the sexual organs as inferior and even disgusting. But even if this attitude was acceptable for a time, it is no longer acceptable today. The time has come to change all these outdated conceptions.

There, that is enough for today; the subject is very vast but I have already said a great deal. If I said more, you would not know what to do with it; it would only burden you. Oh yes, I know: you are always curious to know everything. But the Teaching is not there to satisfy your curiosity! The important thing is to put things into practice and learn to muster your own strength, your own capabilities, and to accomplish some real work. I know very well that you won't like it when I say this, because human beings have been taught to look for what they need outside themselves. This is why your inner centres cannot function as they should; they are too rusty, the currents cannot flow. Of course, there are a few mystics, philosophers and spiritualists who are accustomed to working with their inner resources, but the great majority of human beings are cripples in this respect: they have neither the strength nor the will to work on themselves. This explains why there are so few true Initiates. Even in the East, where there are hundreds and thousands of yogis, saddhus and monks who practise these exercises, very few get any results. Yes, because it is not easy, and the question of reincarnation comes into it too. If you are only just beginning and these centres have been left idle and immobile for centuries, you cannot expect to do much with them. But for those who have already worked at them in previous incarnations and who continue to do so now, the situation is different; they will get some results more easily.

And now, what should you do about it? Start working at it in this incarnation for, if you don't begin now, you will not be able to do so next time, either. You may not obtain any very sensational results, at once, but that does not matter; at least you will have made a start. In your next incarnation you will go on from there, and then you will get substantial results. The important thing is to begin. Success or the lack of it does not matter: what matters is to get the divine currents flowing.

Sèvres, 12 January 1969

II

Question: *Master, we were unable to be at Sèvres at Christmas so we didn't hear what you said about the Hara centre. Could you say something about it now?*

For years now I have been educating you, first and foremost, in the things of the higher spheres, of the divine world of light. But this was in order to prepare you to penetrate into the depths of your own being. For, in order to know one's true self, one has to know both regions: that which is above as well as that which is below. That which is above is the brain, and that which is below is what the Japanese call the Hara centre. And what do they tell us about this centre? That it is the centre, first of all, of a person's equilibrium, and also of his strength, health, power and peace. They have methods by which to awaken and develop this centre and draw energy from it, for it is a storehouse of riches and many entities dwell in it.

If the brain represents Heaven, consciousness, this other centre represents the underworld, the subconscious, the obscure depths of man. These dark regions are, to be sure, very dangerous for anyone who is not strong and well armed, and this is why it is important to begin by exploring the higher ground. Later, when one is really sturdy and in possession of all the necessary arms and equipment, one can go down into the abyss to discover its secrets. The origin and source of life are here, below, but Hell and its monsters are also here. Yes, all the wealth of the world as well as all dangers lie underground. If you want to find gold, precious stones or oil, you have to explore the bowels of the earth, and explorations of that kind require that you take many precautions. In the same way, if someone wants to find gold, precious stones or oil within himself, he is also going to have to take all kinds of precautions; if he does not know how to protect himself and surround himself with light, he will be defeated. Yes, this is why our Teaching begins with the world above so that you will be able, one day, to work with the lower world.

For centuries, theologians have had an attitude of scorn or even disgust for the lower parts of the body. But Nature's opinion on the subject has always been very different, and I am interested in aligning myself with the opinion of Nature, not with that of human beings who are always more or less prejudiced. Nature looks at things quite differently; for her, both the upper and the lower parts are important; in fact, the belly is even more important than the rest. This is obvious from the fact that she always takes care of that aspect first; she is not too concerned with the stupidity or intelligence of human beings as long as they are alive; in other words, it is the belly that matters most. As a matter of fact, if you look around you, you will see that very few people really consider the brain to be the most important. Most human beings attach more importance to their belly and their sexual organs. As long as they can eat and drink and have their pleasures, they don't worry much about the rest! In this, they are closer to Nature for, believe me, Nature is not interested in producing great philosophers, prophets or Initiates; she is only interested in producing living animals who can walk and run, eat and drink and fight each other!

The belly is the zone in which living beings are created and formed: this shows how important it is. There is nothing shameful about it: life would not choose a place of shame in which to be conceived! Of course, it is true that it is not especially beautiful – at least, not according to our notion of beauty – but there must be a reason why life begins there. Not only is the womb in which a mother carries her child, in the belly, but the child draws nourishment and strength into its own belly through the umbilical cord. The Russians call this region *jivot*, and in Bulgarian, *jivot* means 'life'. Yes, this is where life begins and, from here, it radiates and spreads to the other organs. The brain, therefore, also stems from this centre and draws life from it. As we saw before, the most important part of a tree is its roots that are hidden under the ground, obscure and discreetly out of sight. The Hara centre represents our roots. And if we go down into our roots to see what nature has put there, we shall discover a world of the most extraordinary wealth and variety of materials and energies: a veritable mine, an inexhaustible source.

I have already spoken to you of the passage in the Gospels, in which Jesus says, 'Out of his belly will flow rivers of living water'. This shows that Initiates knew the importance of the Hara centre a very long time ago, but they have never talked about it very much because it is too dangerous. They prefer to emphasize Heaven, the virtues, purity and light and say nothing about this centre which stands for the world of darkness. But the alchemists studied the question and spoke, for instance, of 'the light born of darkness'. Darkness is infinitely vaster than light: it embraces, invades and penetrates all things. Light is like a tiny spark wrapped in darkness. All birth comes from the womb of darkness, that is to say, from the invisible world, because the invisible world is the root of being. Every phenomenon on earth, every manifestation or materialization, is simply an expression of the energies and elements that spring from darkness; and, like children in their mother's womb, they are attached to Nature by a kind of umbilical cord through which they draw sustenance from the Cosmic Soul.

Man is no more capable of direct contact with his Hara centre than with his solar plexus, because his conscious thought has no direct access to his subconscious. He can only reach it indirectly, by the way he lives. If his Hara centre is not harmoniously aligned with the universe, therefore, it is because his disordered, chaotic, irrational way of life prevents it from functioning correctly and he is incapable of receiving the emanations of the Universal Soul. The importance of this centre is incalculable, even greater than that of the brain, because the brain can neither produce nor propagate life. Also, the brain is dependent on the energies it receives or fails to receive from the Hara centre. This is why some of the Slavic languages call this centre *jivot*, life. I have never spoken to you about this centre before, because you needed years and years of preparation before you were ready to penetrate, explore and develop it and discover the source of your being. Yes, this is where you will find your source! When I said, 'Don't look for solutions outside yourselves or on the surface. Dig, dig deep and you'll find gold and oil!' it was symbolic. It was a way of saying that this was where you had to dig: in the subconscious.

A few minutes ago I said that nature was not really interested in developing the brains of human beings; it was much more interested in their bellies. Well, this is only partly true. It is true of our purely instinctive, biological nature. But there is another, divine, nature in man, whose goals are completely different[1]. Nature begins by giving man all he needs to develop his biological life, but once he has this, it begins to impose certain limitations on him in order to get him to reflect and learn to make sacrifices and serve others. Animals are given whatever they need, even cruelty, to ensure their survival. But men are curbed and restricted so that they are forced to become wiser and more reasonable and intelligent. Nature does not expect animals to develop those qualities, and yet we are still talking

---

[1] See *Man's Two Natures, Human and Divine*, Collection Izvor, N° 213.

about nature. There are two natures, therefore: a higher and a lower nature. And a disciple is expected to dominate and control his lower nature in order to set his divine nature free. What I said earlier, therefore, is only partly true, for we have to take both natures into account: a lower nature which urges man to eat and drink and reproduce, and a higher nature which, on the contrary, urges him to become a divine, perfect being. And, in order to become perfect, he must start by limiting, restraining some of the elements within him in order to develop others.

Now, to get back to the Hara centre, I also mentioned that the Hindu sacred scriptures said that Brahmâ dwelt below, in the belly. Why has God, the Creator, elected to dwell in such a region? Hermes Trismegistus said, 'That which is below is like to that which is above, and that which is above is like to that which is below'. This comparison is not, as many have thought, a pure fantasy. That which is below is certainly not identical with that which is above. That which is below is like that which is above only in what concerns the importance of the functions; in other words, both below and above, the laws, functions and processes are the same. To say that something is 'like' another is not to say that they are identical.

When you see a house reflected in water, that which is above, in the real world, is like that which is below in the reflected world and vice versa. 'Like' does not mean 'the same matter'. There are two worlds: a world of reflection and illusion, and a world of reality. The world of illusion, which is below, is like the world of reality, which is above but, as in each of the two worlds there is also an 'above ' and a 'below', that which is below in the world of illusion corresponds to that which is above in the world of reality. And since, in the cosmic reality, the Creator is above, in man, who is the reflection of that reality, He is below.

I spoke to you a long time ago about this inversion when I told you that stones, minerals and crystals in the world below, represent the divine world, above. And in man, the belly, which is below, corresponds to what is on high in the Deity, for man, the microcosm, reflects the macrocosm in reverse! This is why Brahmâ, the Creator, is said to dwell in man's belly.

The centre that builds, organizes, nourishes, purifies, strengthens and gives repose, therefore, is this lower centre. We could never get up in the morning if it were not for the tremendous work of physical restoration it achieved during the night. Whereas, more often than not, the brain only manages to get us into hot water!

I have already talked to you about the difference between the intellect and the heart, and told you that the veritable heart is not the hydraulic pump that sends blood racing through the body. Our veritable heart, our spiritual heart, consists of the Hara centre and the solar plexus. Both feeling and understanding are lodged here. Yes, for sensation is understanding, comprehension, but a different form of comprehension; there is nothing intellectual about it. If you cultivate only your intellectual comprehension you will never know anything but the outer aspect of things, you will never see into their depths and vibrate to the splendour of the life that inhabits them. If you want to know the deeper, mysterious, unseen aspects of reality, you must develop the Hara centre; only it will enable you to vibrate in unison with the source of the life that courses through the universe.

One day I will tell you more about this. It is such a profound, sacred reality that the Invisible World will not allow me to reveal everything yet. I am waiting for them to let me know when I may speak. To be sure, I have worked at all this for years, but I cannot speak about it. And there are a great many other things that I cannot talk about until I have experienced and tasted them hundreds of times myself, first.

So, there you have a few words in answer to your question. There are quantities of fascinating things that you still know nothing about, but you never have any time to devote to exploring them. Oh, to be sure, you find plenty of time for things that will make you suffer and complicate your existence. In fact, it seems that these are the only things that count... When are you going to make up your minds to free yourselves and study the marvels of Creation?

Videlinata (Switzerland), 1 March 1969

III

Question: *'Master, will you please tell us how the second birth manifests itself?'*

This is a very important subject, and I have spoken about it several times, particularly in the Christmas season, when our attention is necessarily focused on the birth of Jesus. As I have said, the birth of Jesus has to be interpreted symbolically as the birth of Christ in each individual soul. The physical birth of Jesus, two thousand years ago, is not enough. Christians are proud of this happy event, but they do nothing about it. There are not many who decide to learn and work hard, to put all their efforts into bringing Christ to birth in the souls and spirits of all men. And yet, if it were sufficient for Jesus to have been born two thousand years ago, why has the Kingdom of God not come yet? Why have war, poverty and disease not disappeared yet?

To be sure, the birth of Jesus was an event of the utmost importance... important beyond the power of words to express. I have never said that you should belittle it, but I insist that it must have a continuation in your lives. The birth of Jesus must continue in the religious and mystical dimension. An event of this nature must never cease in time. The Apostles knew that the birth of Jesus must be repeated in each human soul, but this is something that is still not clear in the minds of Christians, in spite of the fact that St Paul said, 'How much have I suffered to bring Christ to birth in you!' But what form does this birth of Christ take? This is an immense question; to answer it one has to know how human beings were constructed in the Lord's workshops.

If you want to study a human being, it is no good thinking that you can weigh and measure him or cut him up in bits to see what is inside. No, if you go about it that way, you will not discover anything; or rather, you will discover a certain number of organs, bones, nerves and capillaries, etc. But you will not discover the man himself, for he is not there. The essence of a man is subtle, invisible, intangible and weightless. This is a very vast subject: you will remember that, in other lectures, I have spoken about man's etheric, astral, mental, Causal, Buddhic and Atmic bodies and explained what kind of matter they are made of, as well as their role and how they function. Orthodox science knows nothing about these bodies, and that is why it is unable to solve so many pedagogical, psychological and medical problems: they remain insoluble because their solution does not depend on physical means or material conditions, but on the knowledge of man's subtle bodies. I have already given several lectures on this subject and I shall certainly speak of it again.

And now let us look at the symbolism of the manger. Why was Jesus born in a manger, on a bed of straw, between an ox and an ass? You will certainly understand in what part of your body the manger is to be found if you remember my lectures about the Hara Centre, in which I quoted this passage from the Gospel: 'Out of his belly will flow rivers of living water'. Why did Jesus have to be born in a stable rather than in a palace, a temple or a vast, sumptuously furnished house? Everything in the Gospels is symbolic, but although Christians have known this story for more than two thousand years, they have never suspected that there was an extremely profound meaning hidden in the account of Jesus' birth in a manger. Also, they think that the Apostles were nothing more than illiterate, ignorant fishermen. Yes, Jesus was blind and picked out his disciples at random! If you only knew who those disciples had been in past incarnations! There were prophets and kings amongst them; in fact one of them had been Solomon. Yes, one of the twelve Apostles had been Solomon, but which one? Naturally, he had lost all his splendour and glory, because he had misused his tremendous wealth to indulge in a life of luxury and voluptuousness. Nevertheless, he had many very noble qualities as well as great knowledge, so he had been given a place close to Jesus. But Christians don't believe in reincarnation and they try to explain everything without reference to it; they will never really explain anything without reincarnation.

But to get back to the question of the second birth: you all know the passage in the Gospel in which Jesus tells Nicodemus, 'Unless a man be born again, he cannot see the kingdom of God'. But Nicodemus was astounded and asked, 'How can a man be born when he is old? Can he enter a second time into his mother's womb and be born?' And Jesus replied, 'Unless a man be born of water and the Spirit, he cannot enter into the Kingdom of God'. Man's second birth, therefore, is a result of the combined work of water and the spirit, that is to say, of water and fire. There are four elements: earth, water, air and fire. Earth, water and air are material elements, whereas fire belongs to the etheric plane. Fire transcends the three states of matter represented by the other three elements. To be sure, fire and light are material, but the matter of which they are composed is so subtle that human beings do not know it: they have never managed to put it into a test-tube and analyse it, for it cannot be studied by physical processes.

Water and fire are symbols and, in the language of symbols, water represents primordial matter, the formless matter that the

Greeks called *hyle*, and fire represents the spirit. When fire and water work together they produce a force which can be harnessed and used by man. With the steam engine, men made a vitally important discovery but, so far, it has only been used to drive machines, trains and ships and that does not really amount to much. Water and fire are the two principles indispensable to the birth of a third principle: energy. Of course, you can give them other names: matter and spirit, for instance, or woman and man, but they are always the two principles, masculine and feminine, which must unite in order to produce the third principle: a child. However, there is one thing that it is important to know in this connection, and that is that if, for instance, you want to produce energy by combining fire and water, you have to keep them apart by putting the water in a kettle or a saucepan. If you throw water directly onto the fire, it will simply evaporate and the fire will be extinguished. And isn't this what happens with many married couples? In their ignorance of how to work together, the wife evaporates and the husband fizzles out!

How to work by combining fire and water: this is what we learn in an Initiatic Teaching. For water and fire are also the heart and the mind, feelings and thoughts. The heart is feminine and the mind masculine, and you have to learn how to work by combining the two, otherwise you will be forever an unproductive bachelor... or spinster! Yes, in this respect almost all human beings are unmarried. Some are all intellect and become as dry as dust. Others are all heart and become so 'damp' that they are full of fog and clouds; there is no light in them! In whatever area of life one looks, it is obvious that human beings have not yet understood how to associate the two principles, fire and water, the emissive and receptive dimension.

And now, if we look for the correspondences on the level of the divine world, we see that fire is wisdom and water is love. The marriage of love and wisdom gives birth to truth, and truth is the birth of Christ, that is to say, the birth of a new consciousness. The first birth is the birth of a baby into the physical world; it is born with arms and legs, a nose, a mouth and lungs and, little by little, it develops and grows, breathes, eats and walks. The second birth is also the fruit of a conception, but this conception takes place in another world, in a world in which the spirit weds with pure matter to conceive a divine child. And when a child is born in the spiritual world, he too can walk and talk and work in that world. So this is the second birth: to enter and live in a universe of another dimension.

When the soul and the spirit unite they bring into the world a seed which grows into a new consciousness. Initiates who have been born a second time are freed from all passions and lusts and from all base desires, and their spirit rises to a great height. But you cannot understand what I am saying: if you yourself have not been born a second time you cannot understand what this second birth is. It cannot be explained. You cannot explain sunlight to a blind man, nor music to someone who is deaf...

When you come to birth for the second time, you will feel it; it will be an event that you will never be able to forget. And this second birth takes place here, in the region of the solar plexus, the navel and the Hara centre. This is the manger, lying between the ox and the ass, that is, between the liver and the spleen. And, on high, there will be music, the song of Angels. Yes, for a second birth is an event in which all Heaven participates. The events that surrounded the birth of Jesus are reproduced each time a human being is born again. The ass, the ox, the three Kings and the Angels... they are all there. This is not something that happened only once, two thousand years ago, in Palestine, it is something that continually repeats itself. Ah, yes, and there are many things one has to know in order to form a child inside oneself: how to carry it, how to nourish it, and so on.

The second birth manifests itself, therefore, in the form of an expanded consciousness, as an inner light that dispels all darkness; as a warmth and love so intense that even if you are abandoned and alone in the world you never feel lonely; as a superabundant life springing up wherever you set foot; as an uprush of forces that you dedicate to building the Kingdom of God, and as joy. Yes, as an extraordinary sense of joy that comes from feeling that you are in communion with the whole universe and all advanced souls, from feeling that you are part of that Immensity, and from the serene conviction that no one can ever steal that joy from you. In India this is the state known as Buddhic Consciousness. This is what Christians call the birth of Christ.

I have never before dared to reveal to you the mystery of this manger in which the second birth takes place. But now you know that this is where Jesus is born, in the depths of the belly, between the ox and the ass, the liver and the spleen. The birth of Jesus in a manger, therefore, has an Initiatic meaning of the utmost importance. It is there, in his Hara centre, that a disciple must bring to birth this new consciousness, the Infant Christ.

When I spoke to you about the Caduceus of Hermes, I said that the two serpents twined round the central staff symbolized the two currents flowing from the brain. Starting from the left and right hemispheres, they cross over at the nape of the neck, pass through the lungs, cross over again at the solar plexus, pass through the liver and spleen, cross over at the navel, pass through the left and right kidneys, cross over once again at the Hara centre and pass through the sexual glands, in a man, and the ovaries, in a woman. As you can see, the liver and spleen lie on the path of these two currents.

To be born of water and the spirit... Initiates, who are familiar with the language of symbolism, do not limit themselves to the two words, 'water' and 'spirit'; they find correspondences and relations between these two realities in every domain of creation. The same laws prevail in every region

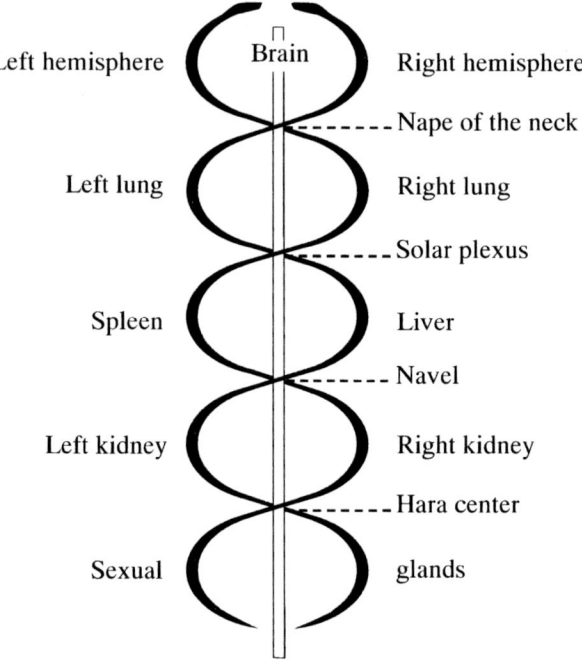

of the universe. If babies are born in the physical world, it means that babies are also born in other worlds. This is why I say that it is not only women, but men, also, who give birth to children. They are not aware of it, but their thoughts and feelings are their children. And the same is true for women. People imagine that children can be born only on the physical plane; no: birth is a phenomenon that occurs in every region of the universe,

I realize, of course, that some people will think that what I am saying is highly implausible, even grotesque! But I am speaking for those who are already working in this direction, who have already made some progress along this path and need only a few indications in order to discover the secret. Thanks to the preceding lectures, you understand, now, in what part of the physical body this birth takes place. You are astounded, I can see that... But, no: Christ will not be born in your heads! Have you ever seen a child born from someone's brain? No one stops to think about that. Some people think that the belly, the womb, is disgusting, and yet the Lord chose this place for the perpetuation of mankind!

Before long you will feel the presence within you of a great light, and you will sense the correspondence that exists between the lower centres (the solar plexus, the navel and the Hara centre) and the three higher chakras, Sahasrara, Ajna and Visuddha, in connection with the eyes, nose and mouth and with love, wisdom and truth. And when you understand the importance and function of these lower chakras, the laws of affinity and analogy will help you to discover, also, how things function on the higher level. And, when this happens, the greatest mysteries of creation and of the spiritual life will unfold before you.

Videlinata (Switzerland), 6 March 1969

Chapter Eleven

THE INITIATIC HEART

'If you know how to use the energies contained in your food, you can transform part of them into a life of such subtlety that it will enable you to touch the heart of the universe.'

As I have already told you, although Initiates never speak of the intelligence of the brain, they are fond of the expression, 'the intelligence of the heart'. Are they so ignorant that they know nothing about anatomy, physiology or psychology? Or do they, on the contrary, know more than biologists and psychologists? Why do they say that it is the heart that is truly intelligent? And what kind of intelligence are they talking about?

When an Initiate speaks of the heart, he is not referring to the organ that pumps blood through our bodies; he is referring to a different heart: the solar plexus. In other lectures I have told you that the solar plexus was a brain in reverse; I explained that it had been formed long before the brain; that, in fact, it was the solar plexus which had given birth to the brain and which continued to nourish it. The solar plexus is an inexhaustible reservoir of wealth and energy and even of knowledge; all our knowledge, our archives, our memory, is stored in the solar plexus. If it is allowed to function without hindrance, the solar plexus is tireless and capable of remedying all the ills of the body, of healing and closing wounds, etc. The trouble is, though, that man has received such false notions and ideas that his conscious life gets in the way of his subconscious life and prevents the solar plexus from manifesting itself properly. It is often prevented from functioning at all and, when it cannot continue to supply energy to the brain, the brain becomes weak and dull.

It is the kind of life we lead, therefore, which gives or denies to the solar plexus the possibility of assuming its functions and restoring everything. And, as I have often said, if human beings suffer from so many nervous ailments today, it is because they give the intellect too much work to do and, as the brain is not built to carry such a weight, it is overburdened and defeated. Once man learns how to put his solar plexus to work, he will be tireless. But this is something that orthodox science knows nothing about and, in the meantime, nervous disease is on the increase because men demand too much of their brain and ignore the solar plexus, the centre just below it, at the navel, or that other centre, lower still, which the Japanese call Hara. Yes, these three chakras are designed to fulfil extraordinary functions which have not yet been revealed.

There are a great many things to be learned, my dear brothers and sisters, but, if you want not only to know them, but to know how to use them and benefit from them, you must begin by living in the right way. Yes, but who attaches any importance to the way they live, nowadays? People are only interested in studying and earning money, and they live very badly, in disharmony and noise, in endless problems and turmoil, in a welter of sexual effervescence... Is it any wonder that everything seizes up and disintegrates? The brain is powerless to remedy the situation for it was not designed for that; it was designed only to show us how and where to direct our energies; it is incapable of making good our physical

The Initiatic Heart

deficiencies. Only the solar plexus can do that. This is why Initiates pay far more attention to their solar plexus than to their brain, and the results are excellent. But this, too, of course, takes a great deal of practice and a lot of hard work.

When you experience an emotion: terror, anguish or love, you don't feel it in your brain or even in your physical heart; you feel it in your solar plexus, which is your true heart. When Initiates say that man's true heart is his solar plexus, therefore, it shows that they know human anatomy and physiology far more thoroughly than modern biologists who see only the material, physical aspects, who have rejected the true reality of human beings. Initiates, on the contrary, are concerned, first and foremost, with the subtle, invisible dimension. Their knowledge is prodigious but they keep much of it secret, they cannot reveal it all. They reveal just a few things and we have to discover the rest for ourselves.

People still do not know what a human being really is nor how he is constructed. Biologists and physiologists can give us a few indications which are useful and even necessary, but they are very far from understanding the essence: that remains unknown and obscure. Go and learn from them, if you like, for what they have observed is very worthwhile, but it is still insufficient. Above all, don't accept their conclusions. Only Initiatic Science can give you the correct conclusions, for it alone embraces the whole of reality.

You have to understand why Initiates speak of 'the intelligence of the heart'. Can the brain, the intelligence of the brain, sense how things function within us? Does it know how the processes of elimination, nutrition, circulation, growth and respiration are effected? Does it know all the chemical, physical, biological and magical processes of the body? No, all these things are quite extraordinarily important and complex, and the brain knows nothing about them. Only the solar plexus knows them because they all stem from and depend on it; it possesses a prodigious, immeasurable intelligence which knows all the processes of the universe because it is at the heart of the universe. Official science is very far from understanding all these truths because it does not hold the key to them. It has chosen to restrict itself to the physical, chemical, electrical and mechanical aspects only, in other words, to the material, objective aspect of reality. But this aspect is only a small part of the whole truth; I shall never tire of telling you this and, one day, it will be universally recognized. I have my own laboratories, I have my own equipment; for years I have been working with instruments that are still unknown and which give me far more accurate information than any physical instrument.

There are methods for working with the solar plexus and if you don't learn to use them, you can go for years without awakening this centre or experiencing the expanded consciousness and the fulfilment that it can give you. You will continue to work only on the level of the brain, but you will gain nothing from contemplating the sun, or from meditation or other exercises, until your solar plexus manifests itself and tells you that your consciousness has, at last, reached the bowels of your being. I could talk to you about this sensation, but what good would it do? It would not mean anything to you; it is something you have to experience for yourself. The intellect is incapable of giving you any idea of it. It is like trying to explain toothache to someone who has never had a toothache in his life, or love to someone who has never been in love. Some things simply cannot be understood until they have been experienced; even if I explained this sensation to you, you would not understand. You must work, work at changing your life, at living harmoniously; only then will you be able to awaken these centres, because the law of these three centres is harmony: it is they that maintain a state of harmony in our physical bodies. This is why, when they are prevented from functioning correctly, illness sets in; they can no longer work to correct the situation because our stupid, disordered life gets in their way.

God has shared out the different powers and abilities: some,

He has given to the brain and others, to the solar plexus. The brain can be a formidable power; in fact it is designed to become extremely potent, but it is the solar plexus that has to supply it with the energies and endurance it needs. The solar plexus and the brain are so intimately connected that either can help or hinder the other. God has not given absolute power to only one of them, just as He has not given absolute power to man... or to woman. No, He has given certain powers to man and others to woman, but these powers are so different that they can only manifest themselves fully when the two principles are united and work in harmony for a single goal. Woman cannot bring to their partnership the gifts that man brings, nor can man bring the same gifts as woman, but when they combine their powers the results are fantastic. And science has not yet discovered how the two 'brains', the solar plexus and the brain in the head, are polarized as masculine and feminine, how they interact and influence each other or the power they have over matter.

And now, my dear brothers and sisters, try to put into practice all the truths that I have revealed to you this summer. Otherwise the Invisible World will rap me over the knuckles and tell me, 'You have been giving too many treasures to people who do nothing with them'! Yes, it is possible that the difficulties I have been having recently are a punishment from Heaven for having revealed too much to people who are negligent. Henceforth, I shall take certain precautions: no one will be allowed to come here unless he has filled in and signed a questionnaire and accepted certain conditions. Too much love... too much trust... Yes, and then, look what happens! I never wanted to take such steps but I am forced to do so. My heart has always played tricks on me, because the heart, you know... You will protest, 'But the heart is so intelligent! You have just been explaining that!' Yes, that is what I said, but we have to understand each other. The heart that is in the solar plexus is never stupid; it is always fully aware of what it is doing. But at the back of the head, in the occipital region, which corresponds to the astral plane, there is another heart which is not the Initiatic heart; on the contrary, it is a bit of a dunce: it is sentimental and naïve and ridiculously trusting. I have a bit of that kind of heart, myself, and it often gets me into hot water!

This may astonish and disappoint you and make you think that I have some terrible faults and failings, but that doesn't matter. My intellect, of course, sees everything very clearly, but it is not often given the chance to guide me or give me orders. It sees the truth, but then my heart says, 'Keep quiet! You must be kind, you must help people and do something for them.' My intellect is not so stupid; in fact it is very lucid and relentless in its judgements and conclusions; this is why I try to soften the impact by calling on my heart. But my heart often gets me into trouble. You see? I have been given an intellect with a terrifying power of analysis, capable of reducing everything to powder and, to make up for this extreme, a heart which also goes to extremes of its own... How can I balance and adjust them?

As you see, I have my own problems. My heart and my intellect are not a very good match. I am always giving my brothers and sisters advice about their marriage, but my own... well, it is better left unsaid! My intellect is married to a heart which has nothing in common with it. If only you could see them, walking, arm in arm, down the boulevard or through the park: they are so different in height and figure, and they are dressed up in such strange clothes and such extraordinary colours, that you would die of laughing. (What a lovely way to die!) But still, they are often very good for each other, they smile and wink at each other and, when the intellect gets carried away, the heart soothes it down. It says, 'Listen to me, darling; why did you have to do that? Don't you know that you have to be kind and tender with people and help them gently?' And when this happens, what turmoil goes on inside! It's indescribable! And then, at other times, if the heart has done something stupid, the intellect scolds it: 'You see? I told you so!

When are you going to stop being so stupid and naïve? Are you going to go on getting me into hot water?' Then the heart is so humiliated that its one idea is to hide, but the intellect pursues it, shaking it up and trying to make it see reason. What scenes! Have you never heard the noise up there, in my cottage, when my intellect is scolding my heart? All the shouts and screams? No, of course, nobody can hear the noise except my invisible friends who rush in and try to calm everything down and make peace. You never knew that such tragi-comical scenes went on, did you? But now you know, and you may think what you please!

In the passage that I read to you at the beginning, it said that if you knew how to transform the energies contained in your food, you could touch the heart of the universe. Why the heart? One often hears the expression, 'He touched my heart', but why the heart? Why not the feet? Or the head? Or the stomach? No, we say that someone touched our heart. Then the question is: 'How does one touch the heart?' When you study, reflect and understand things intellectually, it does not mean that you have touched the heart of the universe, no: this is no more than a preliminary condition. You can only touch the heart of the universe with your own heart. When your heart – your solar plexus – begins to feel and love and live with great intensity, then, yes, you will touch and move the heart of the universe, the heart of God, and the life-giving, illuminating currents, forces and energies of that heart will flood into you. Yes, when you project an immense energy of love from your heart, the laws of affinity and resonance evoke a response from that other heart.

If you want to touch the heart of the universe, you must know, feel and enter into the plans and intentions of the Eternal Lord, the Soul of the Universe. But this cannot be achieved by science or reasoning, because these things belong to a different order; they are on a different wavelength, so the heart of the universe cannot respond to them. In order to touch the heart of the universe you must vibrate on the same wavelength, that is to say, you must emanate the same disinterested love. When your wishes and desires and the things you pray for no longer concern only your own interests but the good of humanity and of the universe as a whole, then your desires are on the same wavelength as the heart of the universe. And as the heart of the universe is the source of all happiness and loveliness, the source of all poetry and music, of all that is splendid and divine, then you receive that life, that happiness and all that splendour: you experience Heaven itself.

You cannot touch the heart of the universe just because you are a renowned scholar with a Chair at the University. You will perhaps reach some human brains, but you will not reach the heart of the universe, because the heart of the universe cannot respond to the brainstorms of intellectuals. As for me, I have a criterion by which I can tell if those who come to the Teaching vibrate in harmony with the heart of the universe, that is to say, whether or not they have learned its language. Do you want to know how I can tell? When I am revealing some great Initiatic truth to you, I can feel that all those who have already worked with the methods of the heart, with the intelligence of the heart, immediately vibrate in harmony, in unison with me. Whereas the others remain unmoved and as cold as ice, as though they were too self-important to vibrate in unison with what I am saying. Yes, and I can see that if they continue to be like that, they will never touch the heart of the universe.

All intellectuals are deformed at the university. I have studied and received degrees from universities, too, but I protected myself; I refused to give way and become like everybody else. And yet, I could have taught at a university, too, if I had wanted to. Why not? I would only have had to work for a few years, because I had already finished courses in psychology, education and philosophy. In fact, I also spent some time studying mathematics, physics, chemistry, medicine and astronomy... not for a degree: just to have the basic notions. I was the eternal student! That is why I finished very late. Everybody said, 'Look at him; he's still a student!' They did not know why I attended all the different Faculties. But once I had finished, I tried to erase from my mind almost everything I had learned, because I saw that it was completely foreign to what I sensed and perceived through meditation and astral projection. Why are others misled by all that?

I know many university professors who would never be able to understand the profound nature of our Teaching because, whatever I revealed to them, whatever I did, even if I brought the stars down to earth, they would always be cold and indifferent; they would never vibrate. This is why I am sure that they will never touch the heart of the universe; at least, not now. They can write books and explain a great many things, to be sure! But they will never touch the heart of the universe... because they themselves have no heart! Oh, of course, they have a heart like everyone else; they can be nice and kind and sentimental, but that heart is not the Initiatic heart. Outwardly, therefore, they may be with us, but, in reality, they are not with us. Why not? Because they cling to their personality; they are incapable of sacrificing it. And what advantages does their personality give them? The approval of a handful of human beings on earth. Ah, yes, that is all they work for: to win the acclaim of a few members of the general public! Whereas we work to win the approbation of the Heavenly entities and, to win this, we have to change our point of view and pay much less attention to the opinion of the masses.

The vast majority are not heroic enough to make up their minds to change their point of view. But when they get to the other side, they will be shown what a mistake that was: they will see that they have failed to understand or earn or build anything worthwhile, all because they clung so obstinately to the criteria of the fifth race, the race of the intellect, and took it as their model and ideal. True, the fifth race has discovered a great deal, but not everything; you must not think that it is the crowning point of creation. The poor creatures are always in the same quandary; there is nothing one can do to help them. In fact, they say it themselves. They say, 'I have studied every subject under the sun. I have learned everything there is to learn, but I vibrate to nothing. The spiritual life says absolutely nothing to me.' Why? Because their brains are too highly developed, they have been too conscientious and taken their studies too seriously; in other words, they conformed too perfectly to the ideal of the fifth race. They never neglected anything that was asked or demanded of them: it was always carried out to perfection. But then, why can't they live the divine life? Precisely because they have been too perfect, too faithful to those external forms. Sometimes that can be an obstacle.

Personally, I was not like that at all. For me, it was half and half. I learned only as much as I needed to get my degree, and spent the rest of my time reading other books and doing exercises of meditation and contemplation. I would go to the University from time to time... but the professors were furious because I was almost always absent. And when it was time for the exams, I went back to my textbooks so as to be able to stammer out some answers. In this way I managed to preserve the spiritual dimension. Fortunately for me! Otherwise I would be just one more learned dunce! For days and nights on end I threw myself, body and soul, into unimaginable spiritual exercises. For me it was a matter of life and death. But I did it all in secret; I never breathed a word to anyone, not even to the Master Peter Deunov. Oh, of course, he watched and studied me, so he always knew what was going on. And, from amongst his forty thousand disciples, he chose the most peculiar and insignificant of them all to come to France! He did not send the cleverest or most learned and erudite; in fact he forbade them to come. Isn't it rather strange that the Master did that?

When I see that you are vibrating in unison, and with all your heart, with the truths by which I live and which I reveal to you, then I know that you will soon find your way to them. If your heart vibrates in harmony with divine truth, Heaven will not let you lose your way. But if you have not got that heart, even if you know everything, Heaven will ignore you. Human beings may acclaim you, of course, but how long will that last? One short incarnation! And then, when you get back to the world above, you will discover that you are not appreciated because, up there, there are no Ph.D's or Professors, or anything else! Up there, you will be considered a kind of unkempt animal because you have never learned to vibrate in unison with the heart of the universe.

Try to understand what I am saying. If you want to touch the heart of the universe, you must be filled with disinterested love and dedicate yourself to an immense, divine idea: the Kingdom of God and His Righteousness. I have already told you this many times: orthodox science and the things you learn in universities and schools, only give you the means to organize your material affairs. The instruction you have received was only designed to make things easier for you in this world, not in Heaven. There are no colleges or universities on earth in which human beings can learn how to live in Heaven, in their own inner Heaven. But how many people are capable of understanding that the only things the fifth race can give them are the means and skills that will help them to get along in this world, to have money and a good job, to gain prestige and renown, to enjoy a life of pleasure or political power; nothing more? In the Universal White Brotherhood, on the other hand, you will not be given the means to become a professor, a magistrate, a Cabinet Minister, a banker or a king, but you will live in Heaven, in light and love... and later, if you are patient, you may well become more than a professor, more than a banker or a Minister, more than a king!

Forgive me for talking to you like this, my dear brothers and sisters, but you need criteria and many of you have not got any. Many of you, in fact, have never looked at yourselves, you don't really know what your attitude is. You are intellectually satisfied; you approve and appreciate what I am saying, but your hearts don't vibrate. Oh, you are not stupid, you are capable of seeing that something is true and logical, sensible and useful or noble, but you don't let your hearts vibrate; you keep them for yourselves. I can feel this attitude in you, and it is not a good one. You should vibrate to what I tell you for, very often, when I talk, it is not I who am speaking. I admit that, personally, I deserve to be cold-shouldered, but you could, at least, let yourselves vibrate with the being who is speaking through me. Yes, for there is someone else behind me who tells you things that even I do not know. After a lecture, some of you come and ask me, 'How did you know? You talked about what has just happened to me.' 'Oh, really?' I say; 'I didn't see anything. I don't know anything about it!' As I have already told you, I am not clairvoyant, but someone else dwells in me, and he sees and hears everything. Yes, it has often happened. I always deny that I had anything to do with it and refuse to take the blame; it is that other being who does it and if you want to blame him for it you are going to have to go and get hold of him and fight it out between you! But leave me out of it. I had nothing to do with it; surely that is clear enough? Yes, it is quite clear... or perhaps it is not clear at all!

Henceforth, meditate on the heart of the universe. Yes, everyone says it: 'He touched my heart.' But how can you touch someone's heart? By producing the same waves, the same vibrations; if you do that you can get whatever you ask for. When you touch someone's heart he opens his doors to you and gives you all he has. Otherwise, you can tell every imaginable tale of woe: 'My wife is expecting a baby; my children are ill; I have done this or that... I belong to this or that organization...' The only answer you will get is, 'Go away', and the door will be slammed in your face. At other times, you say nothing at all; you only look, and you may be given a warm welcome: 'Come in! Come in! Here, have this: it's yours!' Can you explain this? You must find the secret. Do you remember the talk I gave you, one day, about the old-fashioned crystal sets? You can slide your little needle back and forth across the crystal and hear nothing, and yet the needle is in contact with the surface. Yes, but you have not made contact with its heart, for that crystal also has a heart! But as soon as you touch its heart you hear music. And in the universe, also, there is a heart, but we don't know its laws so we can't make contact or get onto its wavelength to receive its signals and the revelations they hold.

In order to touch the heart of the universe you must love with greater intensity. And this is something that happens in the solar plexus. When you do this your mental activity ceases: you project a force, a powerful beam of energy, a strong current of love, and although you are still truly in control, yet your brain remains at rest. You understand, you are fully conscious and you direct your energies without tension or activity of the brain. How is this possible? The explanation is that there is another form of thought, another kind of comprehension, that people in the West have never discovered. But in India, China and Japan, this science has been known for a very long time.

Be patient; we'll come back to the subject another time.

The Bonfin, 30 September 1971

Chapter Twelve

THE AURA

Earlier, when we were in the forest together, I promised to speak to you about the aura.

Several years ago, already, I told you that everything that exists (human beings, animals, plants and even stones) is surrounded by its own subtle, fluidic atmosphere made up of the particles and emanations it is constantly giving off. It is this atmosphere that constitutes the aura. Of course, it is not visible, except to clairvoyants; in fact, a great many people don't even know that it exists. The aura is a kind of halo which surrounds every human being, the only difference being that some people's aura is immense and very brilliant, extending its gloriously varied colours and intense vibrations to great distances, whereas others are meagre and lustreless, with dirty, blurred colours.

I have often compared the aura to the skin of our physical bodies, and you know how vital the skin is for the well-being of our bodies. It serves several important purposes, first amongst them being that of protection: like a shield or a suit of armour, it protects us against blows, sudden changes of temperature and so on. Another function of the skin is to serve as an organ of exchange which absorbs certain elements and eliminates others as it breathes in and out. And finally, the skin serves as a sense organ by means of which we experience sensations of heat and cold, physical contacts, pain, and so on. But I don't want to talk about the functions of the skin: that is not my field. If you want to learn more about it you can look it up in textbooks of anatomy and physiology. What I am interested in today is in drawing a parallel between the skin and the aura, for the aura has the same functions as the skin. The aura is, as it were, the skin of the soul: it surrounds and protects it, serves as a sense organ and, finally, is the means of communication which enables the human soul to receive Cosmic currents and to communicate and exchange with other creatures of the universe, even with the stars in the heavens, and with the Supreme Universal Soul.

  The aura can also be compared to the earth's atmosphere. Yes, this is something extraordinary: the earth also has a protective screen, a skin. The earth's skin is a good deal thicker than ours, of course, but it serves exactly the same purpose. Who knows how often the earth's atmosphere has saved it from destruction during the course of its journey through space? All the meteors that hurtle through space could collide with our planet with catastrophic results if the atmosphere were not there to slow them down and disintegrate them before they reach the earth! And the atmosphere protects us from still other dangers: certain cosmic rays, for instance, which would be deadly for us if the chemical elements contained in the atmosphere were not there to neutralize them.

  Thanks to his aura, a permanent relationship of reciprocal exchange exists between man and the forces of nature. All the cosmic, planetary and zodiacal influences moving through space touch us and, depending on the purity and sensitivity of our aura and the colours it contains, we pick up or fail to pick up certain forces. Our aura, therefore, is like an antenna; it is an instrument which detects and receives messages, waves and forces from the length and breadth of the universe. None of the negative, harmful influences at large in the universe will be able to reach

The Aura

your consciousness or upset or harm you if your aura is very powerful and luminous. Why not? Because, before they can get to you, they come up against your aura. Yes, the aura constitutes an impenetrable barrier, a protective wall. Or you could compare it to a customs house at the frontier between two countries: the customs officers allow no one through without first inspecting their trunks, suitcases and handbags. To be sure, they act without your being aware of it, but they can warn you of danger. So, as you see, although we distinguish the different functions of the aura, in practice they are closely linked: sensitivity, exchange and protection all function at the same time, for the aura is alive.

Now, let's look at the factors which contribute to the quality of our aura: they are exactly the same as those which determine the quality of our skin. There are different types of skin: coarse-grained, rough, dry or, on the contrary, smooth, fine-grained and soft. Almost anyone can judge the quality of a person's skin at a glance, but what gives the skin its particular qualities? The overall physical and psychic condition of the person: man manufactures his own skin.

One day, some years after I had joined his School, the Master Peter Deunov told me, 'You have changed your skin.' Nothing more, just: 'You have changed your skin'! I had no idea what kind of skin I had had before or what kind I had at the time, but I did not ask him to explain. Several years before becoming his disciple, I had flung myself eagerly into various yogic exercises of deep breathing and concentration, and I had really lost my head. I spent days and nights in study, fasting, meditation, concentration and breathing exercises and I had become very thin and pale and weak. My mother was in despair at this son of hers who was interested only in meditation, who never set foot outside the house, who was visibly wasting away and whose friends all laughed at him. She even wanted to burn all my books because she thought that they were the source of all my problems. She begged me to go out into the park, but I was too much in love with my exercises! I was only sixteen and I had found a book by Yoga Ramacharaka which explained all the different breathing methods and what one could gain from them, but without explaining the disorders and problems they could lead to if one embarked on them without the help of a guide. As I had not yet met the Master, I had no one to warn me and I knew nothing about these dangers; I had no sense of moderation. I practised breathing exercises for hours and days on end until, one day – as was only to be expected – I fell ill; so ill that everyone was in a panic, thinking that I was about to depart this world. I was delirious; in fact I had almost left this world... But perhaps I stayed because I still had to suffer here!

The extraordinary thing is that, in my delirium, I kept asking for just one thing: books, books, all the best books. I was not interested in living or in getting well: I only wanted to read all the books in all the libraries of the world! I asked especially for books of philosophy, religion and science, and the only way my poor parents could satisfy me was by bringing me piles of books which they put beside my pillow, so that I could see and touch them. And it was those books that cured me! Yes, but as soon as I was cured, my craze for books disappeared.

It was during my convalescence that I met the Master, and he immediately saw what kind of person I was. Oh, yes: nothing escaped him! Not that he stared at people, of course; he was much too courteous to do that. But sometimes, when you were busy with something, you would feel his eyes on you and, if you turned round, he would pretend not to be watching you. Yes, he was extremely tactful. And yet, I often sensed that he penetrated and searched my innermost being! A few years after meeting him, therefore, when I had already worked very hard and experimented with many things, the Master simply said: 'You have changed your skin.' Naturally, as I say, I did not understand. It was only much later that I understood the importance of the

The Aura

skin, but it was the Master who, unintentionally (or perhaps intentionally?), incited me to study it.

Yes, a person's skin reveals a great deal about its owner. If it is very fine and spiritual it shows that he is a spiritual person, for the skin a person manufactures for himself necessarily corresponds to what he is. Of course, man does not realize that he is responsible for his own skin and that, if he knew how, he could even change it. This is very difficult, of course, but it is possible, and it is extremely important. Man's entire destiny depends on his skin because it has a determining influence on his relations with other human beings and with the outside world. I am telling you this today because I want you to think about it. Every detail of a person's skin means something; even its consistence (smooth, supple, hard, flabby or soft) reflects his essential qualities and characteristics: his perseverance, willpower and activity or, on the contrary, his weakness, laziness and deficiencies.

The skin expresses a man's destiny, all his triumphs and all his failures. You only have to shake someone's hand to discover the essential traits of his character. In fact, if you knew exactly what the physical characteristics corresponded to, you would only have to shake hands once to have a detailed and accurate picture of someone's strengths and weaknesses. But as people shake hands automatically, without paying attention to what they are doing, they never learn anything. We shake someone's hand in order to make contact, to establish a relationship of exchange in which we must give them some of the good that is in us and receive the same from them. If we gain nothing from the gesture, we might as well not do it at all.

But let's get back to the subject of the aura. As I told you a moment ago, the aura is formed by our emanations, and not only the emanations of the physical body, they would not be sufficient to form the aura. The aura is far more complex than that; it is a combination of all the emanations of all our subtle bodies, each of which, by adding its own unique emanations, contributes its own shades and tints to the whole. A man's etheric body forms an aura which penetrates and interweaves with that of his physical body, and the combined aura of his physical and etheric bodies tells you exactly how healthy and vigorous he is. His astral and mental bodies, depending on their activity or inertia, their qualities or their weaknesses, add their own special emanations, their own colouring, to this first aura, thereby revealing the nature of his thoughts and feelings. And the Causal, Buddhic and Atmic bodies, once awakened, add yet other, brighter, more luminous colours and other, more powerful vibrations. The aura, therefore, is a blend of all the different emanations of every aspect of a human being. Just as the earth's atmosphere is permeated with the combined emanations of plants and rocks, of water and mountains and of all the forces flowing from planets and stars, the human aura is a vast, rich synthesis of all that is in man.

As I have said, minerals, plants and animals also have an aura, but theirs is a purely physical aura. Minerals, metals and crystals give off certain forces which form a sort of miniature, coloured magnetic field around them. The aura of plants is more intense and animated than that of minerals. The aura of animals is richer again, because animals have an astral body, the body of desire. Generally speaking, animals have not yet begun to develop their mental body, although biologists do detect a certain capacity for thought in some, such as dogs, horses, elephants, monkeys and dolphins. It is a very rudimentary form of thought, of course, but through constant contact with men, animals begin to develop their mental body; the care and affection of human beings contribute greatly to their evolution. As for human beings, they are developing their mental body at a prodigious rate at the moment; true, they don't always do so in the right direction, but those who know how to guide and control their thought strengthen their auras tremendously.

The Aura

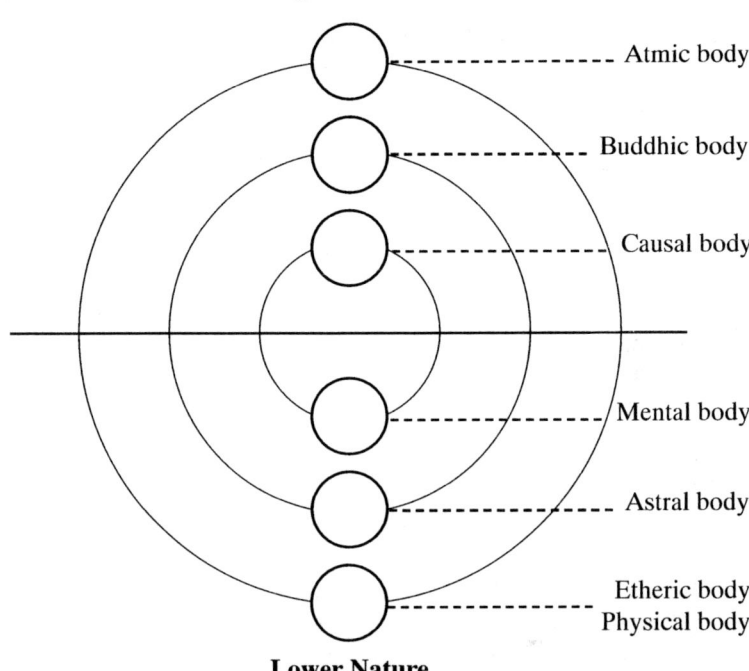

Then there are the Saints, Prophets and Initiates: their attitude of adoration and their love for the Creator cause their Causal, Buddhic and Atmic bodies to form an aura of dazzling splendour in which colours swirl and flow in ceaseless movement, like a glorious display of fireworks. The aura of a Master is immense; it is said, in fact, that Buddha's aura extended for several leagues. Yes, a great Master can project his aura to such great distances that he can take a whole region under his protection and, at the same time, penetrate and intermingle with the aura of all those who live in that region, and breathe new life into them. A Master's one desire is to spread his aura farther and farther, to reach and take 'under his wing' the greatest possible number of human beings. This is his ideal, an ideal of sublime nobility! By means of his aura a

Master purifies the atmosphere and illuminates and gives a new beauty and new life to all creatures. It is through his aura, also, that he influences plants and their seeds and even modifies atmospheric currents. Yes, the aura of an Initiate is something truly divine!

Thanks to the immensity of their aura, which enables them to reach innumerable very remote regions of the universe, Initiates acquire a profound grasp of things. This is why I say that you must stop applying your minds to all kinds of concerns which can give you neither heavenly visions nor heavenly bliss, and launch out on the wings of a strong, luminous aura, to the sublime heights where you may learn how God created the world and what messages He has left inscribed on the stars and the mountains, on lakes, birds, animals and plants. But the one condition that is essential in order to purify, intensify and reinforce your aura, is to cherish the lofty ideal of working at your own perfection, of doing only what is just and noble, of harbouring only the purest thoughts and feelings. If you do this, you will become a focal point of vitality for all around you. When they are with you, people will feel enlightened and calmer and more peaceful.

Those who believe that the time has come to free themselves from antiquated religious and moral codes and, therefore, that the nature of their thoughts, feelings and actions is totally irrelevant, are destroying the beauty of their aura and filling it with drab, dirty colours and chaotic vibrations. Without understanding the reason, people sense this and tend to avoid them. Human beings are drawn to what is pure, luminous and harmonious, so if someone wants to be loved, he is going to have to understand that he must allow only pure, luminous forces to enter him. There is only one way to achieve love, light and power, and that is to work to cleanse your aura of all the impure colours whose bad vibrations destroy the good in others. You have all known people whose presence leaves you emptied and sucked dry after no more than five minutes: all inspiration, joy and faith in God abandon you. Everything bright and good vanishes! But there are others: after only a few minutes in their presence, you feel yourself coming back to life, your old cells are replaced by new ones and, once again, you are full of faith and energy. It is their aura which causes these changes.

Now that you know this, you can readily understand that the aura of an Initiate can be a powerful instrument of magic. Since it is an integral part of his being, wherever he goes, his presence benefits the mineral, vegetable, animal and human reigns. But that is not the end of it: a Master can even use his aura to help the billions upon trillions of disembodied beings in space. Yes, his aura can even reach and help beings in the world beyond. I have given much study to this question and I can tell you that a Master is constantly at work to improve the lot of countless beings in the astral and mental worlds. Even though, on earth, he may have only a handful of human beings in his care, on the other side he is constantly in touch with a multitude of creatures who gather round him to receive warmth, light and renewed life from his aura in order to advance their evolution. Yes, the veritable field of action of the great Masters is not on earth, amongst human beings. Although it cannot be seen by human eyes, their most intense activity takes place on the other side.

The great Masters, who have achieved their ideal of serving God with all their hearts and souls and minds, have awakened their Causal and Buddhic bodies, and it is the vibrations of these sublime bodies that can reach even the creatures on other planets. In the same way, Masters who dwell on other planets reach the creatures on earth and, in this way, there is a continual flow of exchange, not only within the solar system, but throughout the whole cosmos. God has placed no boundaries or frontiers in the universe, and if love is said to be all-powerful it is because it can reach to the stars and touch even the most distant entities. As you can see, the aura is extremely important. If your aura is not pure, the countless blessings poured out by angelic beings cannot enter you because your true self is hidden under dense layers of impurities. When there is a heavy layer of cloud, it hides the sun so that it can no longer give warmth or light to creatures on earth. This is exactly what happens to those who are full of jealousy, hatred and anger, etc.: dense clouds build up in their aura. Actually, the vibrations of the aura are infinitely subtle. It is constantly stirring with rapid movements, ceaselessly and faithfully reflecting the smallest changes in our state of mind and even in our physical condition. True, the aura is constant in that it always manifests the fundamental nature of its owner, but subtle variations continually flit through it. It is like your face: in the course of a day, every possible expression flits across it, but that does not mean that your nose, forehead or mouth actually change shape. In the same way, the aura is made up of certain radiations and colours which reveal a person's true nature, and this does not change substantially during his lifetime, but other, secondary vibrations come and go, reflecting passing changes and states of mind.

Those who give themselves up to certain emotions or weaknesses, therefore, constantly obscure the atmosphere of their aura, so that when beneficial currents and forces seek to enter and find a resting place in them, they are halted by a veritable wall of muddy, opaque colours. If you live an unreasonable, chaotic life, your aura will be criss-crossed by so many untidy eddies and currents that it will no longer be an effective shield against hostile attack by invisible creatures. And it follows that your relationships of mutual exchange with the universe and other living creatures will not be harmonious either. In keeping with the law of affinity, you will receive from the universe only sombre, chaotic and discordant elements; all that is luminous will be rejected. Light attracts light; purity attracts purity. If your aura is impure, drab and chaotic all the pure, harmonious, luminous forces will stay outside and only those that are drab and ugly will enter you, because your aura only lets in forces of the same breed as itself. As we say in Bulgaria: 'Mangy mules can smell each other seven hills

The Aura

away'... Yes, and they are eager to be in each other's company!

If your aura is not luminous, therefore, it is not an effective protection, nor is it a good instrument with which to receive signals from the Invisible World and perceive the hidden aspect of reality; you will possess neither intuition nor foresight; you will be cut off from all exchanges with Heaven; entities dwelling in distant regions of space will not even notice your existence. If you give off no light, those who dwell in the upper reaches of the Invisible World will not see you. If, on the other hand, your aura is luminous, they will see you perfectly. How? Well, suppose you are on a ship in the middle of the ocean at night; if your ship is not carrying lights no one will be able to see it, but if you send up a flare or switch on a searchlight, someone will see you at once and will be able to communicate with you. This is only an example, of course, because there are so many different means of communication nowadays, but it gives you some idea of what I am trying to get you to understand. The world is like an ocean and we are little boats sailing through the night. We are in utter darkness and, if we don't switch on a light of some kind, invisible beings, Angels and Archangels, won't see us. So we have to send out beams of light, and it is our aura which does this. Someone who has a very luminous aura, therefore, can be seen by those who work in the heavenly spheres and, if he calls on them for help, they can find him at once, thanks to the light of his aura. This, too, is no more than an image for, as you can well imagine, if the angelic spirits want to find someone, they have more than one way of doing so! The world has always been described as a vale of tears, suffering and darkness. Yes, and is it surprising that nobody notices or comes to their rescue when human beings groan and cry out in pain and curse their fate? They don't produce any light! They must send out signals of light, and the aura is the instrument that they should use to do so.

Why do you suppose that saints have always been portrayed with halos round their heads? There was once a highly developed science of colour which taught that each virtue was expressed by a particular colour and that the colours produced by these virtues formed the aura. Saints are beings of great purity whose overriding desire is to draw closer to God and to melt into Him in order to know and resemble Him. Thanks to this burning desire to know God, they acquire such deep insight and such great wisdom, that a golden yellow light springs from their innermost being and enfolds them in its glory. There are many different shades of yellow, ranging from the palest, most delicate tints to a strong golden yellow. Each shade and tint has its own special meaning and a great deal could be said about this, for it touches on the alchemical problem of how to transform matter into fluidic gold.

If a disciple fails to protect himself by cultivating certain inner qualities and virtues, enemies will steal into him and he will be unable to get rid of them. How can he protect himself? By working to develop the purity, brightness, beauty, power and magnitude of his aura. Each of these aspects depends on the virtues he cultivates. If a man is pure, his aura becomes limpid and transparent; if he is intelligent, it becomes brighter and more luminous; if he lives with great intensity, his aura will also vibrate with intensity; if he has developed his will-power, it becomes very powerful, and if he concentrates all his energies on spiritual things, his aura expands and grows and becomes immense. And the beauty of the aura, the beauty of its colours, depends on the harmony which reigns amongst his different qualities and virtues.

Those who always think good thoughts, therefore, who possess faith, hope, kindness and purity, receive the rich gifts of nature, and evil can no longer penetrate their defences. They are protected as though by a shield. In fact, the shield with which the knights in fairy tales defend themselves is a symbol of man's aura. And the sword? The sword is the light that radiates from him. There are two symbols here: the protective screen of the aura that surrounds us, represents the feminine principle, and the thought we project, or the spirit darting out into space, represents the active, dynamic, masculine principle. So these two symbols, sword and shield, which can be traced back to the earliest ages of mankind, represent the two principles: the passive principle, the aura, and the active principle, the thought sustained by will, which flashes out like an arrow. As you know, a sword, arrow or spear, has always been seen as the symbol of the active masculine principle. In astrology, the figure of Sagittarius shooting his arrows into the air is a symbol of the Initiate who draws his bow and shoots his thoughts, his mental arrows, to defend the city of the Initiates from invasion by its enemies.

There is no more effective protection than a pure, luminous aura. Of course, all the magic objects, figures and formulas mentioned in esoteric tradition, have their value, they all have their own profound meaning. But no formula or talisman is as powerful as the aura. Before calling on the spirits – particularly if he is addressing spirits of darkness – a Magus draws a circle round himself in which he inscribes the names of God or certain symbols. This circle represents the aura. No man can command the spirits of darkness with impunity unless he is surrounded by a strong protective circle, a powerful aura. In general, in fact, it is true to say that one cannot achieve any substantial spiritual results unless one is surrounded by a protective circle, that is to say, by an aura composed of divine forces and virtues. The names of God inscribed in the magic circle symbolized these virtues.

But a great many people dabble in magic without knowing the origin of the symbols they use or the real meaning of what they are doing. They are content to perform the rites prescribed in their books, oblivious of the fact that it is within themselves that they should trace a circle and inscribe the names of God; in other words, it is within themselves that they must inscribe the virtues that will give them an aura of purity, holiness, light and love. They know nothing of this, so they remain highly vulnerable in spite of the circle they draw, because they draw it only externally; they do not have the qualities they need within themselves to be protected.

When we are told that a Magus places himself inside a circle, with a sword or wand in his hand, and reads a formula from a book, it is all perfectly true. But, for an Initiate, each one of these details corresponds to something that he must already possess in himself. First of all, an Initiate must possess his own inner magic wand, his own inner sword, and his own inner book of formulas. He reads, and the book from which he reads is his knowledge of all the forces and spirits of nature. The magic wand or sword represents the inflexible will-power that he must bring to his work. If he does not possess that wand it means that he does not possess the will-power he needs, and he will be unable to command the spirits. There is no more potent magical instrument than a pure, luminous aura. Write that down: it is important. You must have your own inner magic instruments first of all and, once you have them, you can have as many external instruments as you like. There, I think that that is enough for one day. What I have said should give you a good deal to think about, and you will find other explanations for yourselves.

The thing that women are interested in is love; men, too, of course, but men are more interested in power and knowledge. If women want to be loved, therefore, I have a word of advice for them. No, I am not going to advertise a talisman, prepared by means of magic formulas, or a perfume to bewitch and attract admirers. I am going to reveal a tremendous secret to them (and I'm not asking for a penny: it is all free!). What I have to tell them is this: 'Do you want to be loved? If so, work at your aura! Nourish it, reinforce it, purify and illuminate it. And you will see the results: everyone will love you. But I must warn you of the dangers involved: your aura must be absolutely impenetrable; if you leave even the slightest gap in the circle, you will be vulnerable. Mischievous spirits will be able to get in and your stronghold will be captured.' That is what I want to say to women. It is absolutely normal and good that women should want to be loved; in fact, I advise them to try to be loved. But when someone loves them they must use his love only to help him to accomplish great deeds. Sometimes, a girl is so moved and charmed by a young man's love, that she surrenders and gives herself to him completely. No, she should say: 'The circle is there and I can't let you in at once. Take the fruits of my tree, but the tree is mine. I can't give it to you. I'll give you its fruits; I'll give you my songs; I'll give you the music of my violin, that is to say, my words, thoughts and glances, but I'll keep my tree, my violin, for myself.' This is what she should say.

If you give away your violin to someone who does not know how to play it, he will damage it and then you will have a violin no longer. And if you transplant your tree into your neighbour's garden, you will not have a tree any longer, either. Give your fruits, give your songs, but keep your tree and your violin. In other words, keep your heart and your mind. This is the way of wisdom! But, more often than not, a girl is so entranced by a young man's love, that she is ready to surrender her tree and her violin at once. And then, the young man, who has so easily obtained what he wanted, no longer loves her; that is what is so sad.

Now, how can you develop and improve your aura? There are two possibilities: the first is by a deliberate, conscious effort of mental concentration. You concentrate mentally on colour, and picture yourself bathed in the purest, most luminous colours. To have an accurate idea of the seven colours, you will need a prism, for the colours one sees in nature, in flowers or birds, for instance, are never exactly the true colours of the spectrum. Whereas with a prism you can see true reds, oranges, yellows, greens, blues and purples. Then, in your imagination, you can picture all these colours radiating from you and spreading out into space; picture yourself bathed in that light, in all those glorious colours; imagine that you are surrounded by a bright, shining sphere of light and that you are sending love out into the whole wide universe. An exercise like this can give you such delight that, once you have begun, you may never want to stop!

The second method consists in concentrating all your efforts on acquiring the virtues: purity, patience, indulgence, generosity, kindness, hope, faith, humility, justice and disinterestedness. This second method is by far the most reliable: your work consists in cultivating the virtues, and it is the virtues themselves that form your aura. Of course, the best solution of all is to combine both methods. If you cultivate the virtues, your aura will develop spontaneously and naturally; by a conscious work of the imagination, it will also develop, but less effectively, for if, for instance, you concentrate on your aura every day and, at the same time, continue to live a very ordinary kind of life and break many of the divine laws, you would be building something lovely with one hand and tearing it down with the other. So the best is to combine both methods: live a life of honesty, purity and love and, at the same time, use your powers of thought to work at the embellishment of your aura.

As I have already told you, gradually, as your aura develops, it enables you to communicate with every region in space. If you study the planets of the solar system you will see that, although they are millions of miles apart, they are actually in contact with each other; they form a whole. Yes, if we think that they are separate units, it is because we see only the outward appearances. Take the example of the earth: the continents cover a good deal of the surface, but the oceans cover even more, there is more water than land. The atmosphere, on the other hand, surrounds the earth with a layer of gaseous matter that is several times the volume of the planet, and beyond the atmosphere lie the earth's etheric, astral and mental bodies, which are still more voluminous. For the earth is a living, intelligent being with its own soul and spirit, and if you remember that this is also the case with the other planets, you will begin to see how they all intermingle and penetrate each other. Their physical bodies are very far from each other, but their auras and emanations touch and join. This explains the planetary influences known to astrology: by means of their auras, the planets penetrate and influence each other and all those who inhabit them.

There are still many aspects of the aura which I have not explained, but what really matters is that you learn to care for your aura just as you care for your skin. You have a bath or shower and wash every day, don't you? When it comes to the aura, of course, it's a little more complicated: I don't advise you to apply raw steak or slices of cucumber in the hope of making it soft and smooth! Besides, these things don't really do your skin much good either. Some women never wash their face with water, for instance, in the belief that it is bad for the skin. But there is nothing better than water! Don't apply too many creams and lotions. Some of them are even dangerous: you never know what gets into you through the pores of your skin.

People nowadays always try to improve outward appearances but, in the future, mankind will attach more importance to the inner reality and, instead of going to the beauty salons of earth, women will go to their own spiritual 'beauty salons', by which I mean that they will cultivate and care for their aura. Yes, the aura is the only authentic beauty salon. An intense, luminous aura bestows beauty on its owner, and a beauty that lasts; whereas a woman who has just come from a beauty salon may look a perfect picture, but twenty-four hours later she'll have to begin all over again! And the reason is simply that the improvement didn't come from within, and nothing that does not come from within can last.

The particles emanating from a great Master are alive, intense, luminous and potent. When they penetrate our aura they enter into our very structure and transform our whole being.

Those who receive their Master's emanations with love begin to think and behave like him and, one day, they become as free as he is. To be sure, this does not happen all at once: it takes years and years, but it does happen. Unfortunately, people are not interested in what is invisible. They rely exclusively on what they can see or touch. They neglect the unseen aspects of reality completely, and yet that aspect is so important!

Let me give you an example: picture a scholar who always has his nose in a book; a regular bookworm! He spends his days reading old parchments in a library, and ends by becoming as thin and dried up as they are. And then, one day, he meets a pretty little 'book' in the street, a gay, walking, living book, and he says to himself, 'That's the book for me!' and, there and then, he makes up his mind to read that book. It is a very quiet little book; it is too shy to say much, but that does not matter, he follows it anyway, because it makes him so happy to breathe its emanations! What does all this mean? Ah, the little 'book' is a girl; he does not learn much from her because she is not at all learned, she is no philosopher, no orator, but something fragrant and delicious and enchanting emanates from her. Before long, the bookworm's colleagues notice that he is often absent from the library. And when they do see him, he is almost unrecognizable: he is rejuvenated, there is life in his eyes, his step is springy. Before, he was like a bent old man, shuffling along with his eyes on the ground, and now he has become a poet and counts the stars in the sky. What a transformation! You see? Isn't it wonderful? What an effect fluidic emanations can have! Much more effect than books, because people abandon books in order to contemplate a ravishingly lovely young girl who says nothing. Oh, I know: it is a funny example, but it will help you to understand the power of fluids and emanations, and to understand that, from now on, you must work much more at this aspect of things.

Make up your minds, therefore, to cultivate your aura, and you will find that you begin to understand many things. When

The Aura

you are angry you are steeped in a fiery red, a dark, dirty red, very unlike the rosy red of love. And if you lack faith, if you are not at peace in yourself, you will have a dull, ugly shade of blue in your aura, whereas, as your faith becomes stronger, the blue of your aura becomes as bright as the sky. One day I will talk to you at greater length about the meaning of each colour[1].

And now, try to do an exercise with colours every day: get yourself a prism (you can probably find one in a shop), hold it up to the sun and observe how the white light of the sun is refracted into seven colours as it passes through it. And when you have gazed at the colours for a while, close your eyes and imagine that you are surrounded by purple, then blue, green, yellow and so on. Or you can start with red and end with purple, keeping each colour wrapped round you, as it were, for several minutes. If you do this every day, you will purify and strengthen your aura and find yourself in such splendid form that you will be amazed. Also, if you want to help one of your family or friends who is ill or unhappy and discouraged, do the same exercise for them. Send them the most beautiful colours of the spectrum. Yes, there are a great many things you can do with the aura and the seven colours!

And now, just a few words to conclude: you can do all these exercises with colour when you go up to the sunrise in the morning. Looking at the sun and its aura and all the colours pouring from it into space, say to yourself, 'I'm going to be like the sun. I'll surround myself with rays of light: golden, blue, purple or green light...' Then, spend a long time steeping yourself in the splendour of those colours; contemplate them, picture them reaching to a great distance, so that every living creature is bathed in this marvellous atmosphere, swimming in light, drenched in light... and your aura will be a blessing for all creatures. Yes, you can do this; it is possible. There are no limits to what you can do; it is human beings who impose limits on

---

[1] See *Complete Works*, vol. 10, chap. 11.

themselves. You must have an insatiable appetite for good. Promise yourself, 'I will do it; I will succeed!' A spiritual Master or a disciple who is already very advanced, radiates love to the whole of creation, to the whole universe. His love reaches farther than the stars. Yes, for some this is a reality; they send their love to the stars, and the stars send back a floodtide of love which breaks over them like an ocean wave and they find themselves swimming in love. Cosmic love is their very environment.

Les Monts-de-Pully (Switzerland), 22 May 1960

Books by Omraam Mikhaël Aïvanhov
(translated from the French)

Complete Works
Volume 1 – The Second Birth
Volume 2 – Spiritual Alchemy
Volume 5 – Life Force
Volume 6 – Harmony
Volume 7 – The Mysteries of Yesod
Volume 10 – The Splendour of Tiphareth
    The Yoga of the Sun
Volume 11 – The Key to the Problems of Existence
Volume 12 – Cosmic Moral Laws
Volume 13 – A New Earth
    Methods, Exercises, Formulas, Prayers
Volume 14 – Love and Sexuality (Part I)
Volume 15 – Love and Sexuality (Part II)
Volume 17 – 'Know Thyself' Jnana Yoga (Part I)
Volume 18 – 'Know Thyself' Jnana Yoga (Part II)
Volume 25 – A New Dawn:
    Society and Politics in the Light of Initiatic Science (Part I)
Volume 26 – A New Dawn:
    Society and Politics in the Light of Initiatic Science (Part II)
Volume 29 – On the Art of Teaching (Part III)
Volume 30 – Life and Work in an Initiatic School
    Training for the Divine
Volume 32 – The Fruits of the Tree of Life
    The Cabbalistic Tradition

Brochures:
301 – The New Year
302 – Meditation
303 – Respiration
304 – Death and the Life Beyond

By the same author:
(Translated from the French)

Izvor Collection
201 – Toward a Solar Civilization
202 – Man, Master of his Destiny
203 – Education Begins Before Birth
204 – The Yoga of Nutrition
205 – Sexual Force or the Winged Dragon
206 – A Philosophy of Universality
207 – What is a Spiritual Master?
208 – Under the Dove, the Reign of Peace
209 – Christmas and Easter in the Initiatic Tradition
210 – The Tree of the Knowledge of Good and Evil
211 – Freedom, the Spirit Triumphant
212 – Light is a Living Spirit
213 – Man's Two Natures: Human and Divine
214 – Hope for the World: Spiritual Galvanoplasty
215 – The True Meaning of Christ's Teaching
216 – The Living Book of Nature
217 – New Light on the Gospels
218 – The Symbolic Language of Geometrical Figures
219 – Man's Subtle Bodies and Centres
220 – The Zodiac, Key to Man and to the Universe
221 – True Alchemy or the Quest for Perfection
222 – Man's Psychic Life: Elements and Structures
223 – Creation: Artistic and Spiritual
224 – The Powers of Thought
225 – Harmony and Health
226 – The Book of Divine Magic
227 – Golden Rules for Everyday Life
228 – Looking into the Invisible
229 – The Path of Silence
230 – The Book of Revelations: a Commentary
231 – The Seeds of Happiness
232 – The Mysteries of Fire and Water
233 – Youth: Creators of the Future
234 – Truth, Fruit of Wisdom and Love
235 – 'In Spirit and in Truth'
236 – Angels and other Mysteries of The Tree of Life
237 – Cosmic Balance, The Secret of Polarity
238 – The Faith That Moves Mountains

By the same author:

Daily Meditations:
A thought for each day of the year
A volume published every year

Life Recordings on Tape
KC2510 AN – The Laws of Reincarnation
          (Two audio cassettes)

Videos (french/english)

V 4605 FR – *The Activity of the Soul and Spirit:*
How They Can Manifest Through Us.
How Can We Modify our Destiny?
L'activité de l'âme et de l'esprit et notre travail pour qu'ils se manifestent à travers nous.
Comment peut-on changer sa destinée?

V 4606 FR – *How Can We Purify our Physical Body*
Despite the Pollution of the Atmosphere and Food?
Comment peut-on purifier le corps physique malgré la pollution de l'air et de la nourriture?

World Wide - Editor-Distributor
Editions PROSVETA S.A. - B.P. 12 - F- 83601 Fréjus Cedex (France)
Tel. (00 33) 04 94 40 82 41 - Fax (00 33) 04 94 40 80 05
Web: **www.prosveta.com**
e-mail: **international@prosveta.com**

Distributors

AUSTRALIA & NEW ZEALAND
SURYOMA LTD - P.O. Box 798 – Brookvale – N.S.W. 2100
e-mail: info@suryoma.com – Tel. and fax (61) 2 9984 8500

AUSTRIA
HARMONIEQUELL VERSAND – A- 5302 Henndorf am Wallersee, Hof 37
Tel. / fax (43) 6214 7413 – e-mail: info@prosveta.at

BELGIUM & LUXEMBOURG
PROSVETA BENELUX – Liersesteenweg 154 B-2547 Lint
Tel (32) 3/455 41 75 – Fax 3/454 24 25 – e-mail: prosveta@skynet.be
N.V. MAKLU Somersstraat 13-15 – B-2000 Antwerpen
Tel. (32) 3/231 29 00 – Fax 3/233 26 59
VANDER S.A. – Av. des Volontaires 321 – B-1150 Bruxelles
Tel. (32) 27 62 98 04 – Fax 27 62 06 62

BULGARIA
SVETOGLED – Bd Saborny 16 A, appt 11 – 9000 Varna
e-mail: svetgled@revolta.com – Tel/Fax: (359) 52 23 98 02

CANADA
PROSVETA Inc. – 3950, Albert Mines – North Hatley (Qc), J0B 2C0
Tel. (819) 564-8212 – Fax. (819) 564-1823
in Canada, call toll free: 1-800-854-8212
e-mail: prosveta@prosveta-canada.com / www.prosveta-canada.com

COLUMBIA
PROSVETA – Avenida 46 n° 19 - 14 (Palermo) - Santafe de Bogotá
Tel. (57) 232-01-36 – Fax (57) 633-58-03

CYPRUS
THE SOLAR CIVILIZATION BOOKSHOP
73 D Kallipoleos Avenue - Lycavitos – P. O. Box 4947, 1355 – Nicosia
Tel: 02 377503 – 09 680854

CZECH REPUBLIC
PROSVETA – Ant. Sovy 18, –České Budejovice 370 05
Tel / Fax: (420) 38-53 00 227 – e-mail: prosveta@iol.cz

GERMANY
PROSVETA Deutschland – Postfach 16 52 – 78616 Rottweil
Tel. (49) 741-46551 – Fax. (49) 741-46552 – e-mail: prosveta.de@t-online.de
EDIS GmbH, Mühlweg 2 – 82054 Sauerlach
Tel. (49) 8104-6677-0 – Fax.(49) 8104-6677-99

GREAT BRITAIN – IRELAND
PROSVETA – The Doves Nest, Duddleswell Uckfield, – East Sussex TN 22 3JJ
Tel. (44) (01825) 712988 - Fax (44) (01825) 713386
e-mail: prosveta@pavilion.co.uk

GREECE
PROSVETA – J. Vamvacas
Moutsopoulou 103 – 18541 Piraeus
HOLLAND
STICHTING PROSVETA NEDERLAND
Zeestraat 50 – 2042 LC Zandvoort – e-mail: prosveta@worldonline.nl
HONG KONG
SWINDON BOOK CO LTD
246 Deck 2, Ocean Terminal – Harbour City – Tsimshatsui, Kowloon
ISRAEL
Zohar, 42, Chdérotte Hatsvi, 34355 Haïfa
ITALY
PROSVETA Coop. – Casella Postale – 06060 Moiano (PG)
Tel. (39) 075-8358498 – Fax 075-8359712
e-mail: prosveta@tin.it
NORWAY
PROSVETA NORDEN – Postboks 5101 – 1503 Moss
Tel. 69 26 51 40 – Fax 69 25 06 76
e-mail: prosveta Norden - prosnor@online.no
PORTUGAL & BRAZIL
EDIÇÕES PROSVETA – Rua Passos Manuel, n° 20 – 3e E, P 1150 – Lisboa
Tel. (351) (21) 354 07 64
PUBLICAÇÕES EUROPA-AMERICA Ltd
Est Lisboa-Sintra KM 14 – 2726 Mem Martins Codex
e-mail : prosvetapt@hotmail.com
ROMANIA
ANTAR – Str. N. Constantinescu 10 - Bloc 16A - sc A - Apt. 9,
Sector 1 – 71253 Bucarest
Tel. (40) 1 679 52 48 - Tel./ Fax (40) 1 231 37 19
e-mail : antared@pcnet.ro
RUSSIA
EDITIONS PROSVETA S.a.r.l
Riazanski Prospekt 8a, office 407 – 109428 Moscou
Tel / Fax (7095) 232 08 79 – e-mail : prosveta@online.ru
SPAIN
ASOCIACIÓN PROSVETA ESPAÑOLA – C/ Ausias March n° 23 Ático
SP-08010 Barcelona – Tel (34) (3) 412 31 85 - Fax (34) (3) 302 13 72
aprosveta@prosveta.es
SWITZERLAND
PROSVETA Société Coopérative – CH - 1808 Les Monts-de-Corsier
Tel. (41) 21 921 92 18 – Fax. (41) 21 922 92 04
e-mail: prosveta@swissonline.ch
UNITED STATES
PROSVETA U.S.A. – P.O. Box 1176 – New Smyrna Beach, FL.32170-1176
Tel / Fax (904) 428-1465
e-mail: sales@prosveta-usa.com – web page: www.prosveta-usa.com
VENEZUELA
BETTY MUÑOZ – Las Mercedes, Calle Madrid – Quinta Monteserino – D. F. Caracas
Tel. (58) 014 22 36 748
e-mail : miguelclavijo@hotmail.com

Achevé d'imprimer en avril 2001
sur les presses numériques
de l'Imprimerie Maury SA
21, rue du Pont-de-Fer – 12100 Millau
N° d'imprimeur : D01/25246 H

Dépôt légal : avril 2001